Express Lane COOKING

80 QUICK-SHOP MEALS USING 5 INGREDIENTS

SHAWN SYPHUS

FOUNDER OF THE BLOG, I WASH...YOU DRY

PAGE STREET
PUBLISHING CO.

PAGE STREET
PUBLISHING CO.

First published in 2015 by
Page Street Publishing Co.
27 Congress Street, Suite 103
Salem, MA 01970
www.pagestreetpublishing.com

Distributed by Macmillan; sales in Canada by The Canadian Manda Group.

18   17   16   15   2   3   4   5

ISBN-13: 978-1-62414-114-0
ISBN-10: 1-62414-114-5

Library of Congress Control Number: 2015930606

Cover and book design by Page Street Publishing Co.
Photography by Shawn Syphus

Printed and bound in China

Page Street is proud to be a member of 1% for the Planet. Members donate one percent
of their sales to one or more of the over 1,500 environmental and sustainability charities
across the globe who participate in this program.

TO CHRIS, MY BEST FRIEND
AND ROCK, I LOVE YOU. TO KAYLEE,
CREW, EMMA AND TWILA,
MY FAVORITE TASTE TESTERS,
YOU ARE THE JOYS OF MY LIFE.

CONTENTS

INTRODUCTION

Once upon a time, back in May of 2010, *I Wash...You Dry* was born. At the time I had three small children at home. Between play dates, bike rides and your typical mom duties, my time in the kitchen was always limited. As much as I love to cook, spending my whole day in the kitchen is not my idea of fun. I don't believe that recipes need to be difficult and/or time consuming to be great. That's why my blog's focus has always been to create simple and easy recipes *that taste phenomenal,* all while using as few dishes as possible—'cause seriously, who enjoys doing dishes?! Not me!

Now that I have four kids at home, my theory that dinners need to be quick and easy has expanded into also needing to be versatile. That's how the idea for *Express Lane Cooking* came to be. When I would take my youngest two girls to the grocery store, sometimes I would only have mere minutes before the toddler meltdowns would transpire. I would have to book it out of there with just a few ingredients in hand. It's happened to all of us, *right?* With this cookbook, you'll be able to grab 5 ingredients, and I'll show you how to make 3 different meals that your whole family will love!

My goal is that you'll become more confident in the kitchen and be able to look at the ingredients you have on hand and make something amazing with them. I really hope you enjoy the recipes I've created here for you. You can find more delicious, quick and easy recipes on my blog www.iwashyoudry.com. I hope you'll come say hi!

Now, let's get in the kitchen and start cooking!

—Shawn Syphus

Shawn Syphus

KEEPING A WELL-STOCKED KITCHEN

If there's one thing that can help you become an inspired chef, it's a well-stocked kitchen. When you're working with limited fresh ingredients, having a well-stocked spice drawer, pantry and refrigerator can make all the difference. Here's a list of the different items that I believe you should keep on hand at all times.

SPICE DRAWER

The good news about dried herbs and spices is that, when stored properly, they can last for a long time—*up to three years*! The best place to store your spices is away from heat and light. So while it may seem convenient to keep them right by your stovetop, consider a location a little farther away, like an upper kitchen cabinet.

- Salt—*I prefer sea salt, and use a grinder to crush it.*
- Pepper—*I also prefer to use a triple peppercorn blend and grind my own fresh pepper.*
- Garlic Powder
- Onion Powder
- Ground Ginger
- Chili Powder
- Cayenne Pepper
- Red Pepper Flakes
- Paprika
- Smoked Paprika
- Cumin
- Italian Seasoning Blend
- Dried Oregano
- Dried Parsley
- Dried Basil
- Bay Leaves
- Nutmeg
- Cinnamon
- Vanilla Extract

PANTRY

When I was traveling across the country with my family in our 5th wheel trailer, I still made it a priority to have a well-stocked pantry. I stuck containers of flour, sugar and oats behind the couch, and jars of honey under the kids' beds. These items don't have as long of a shelf life as the spice drawer, but when stored properly can last several months. So whether you have a walk-in pantry or just a couple shelves of cupboard space, these are the things you need to make room for.

- Flour—*I prefer an all purpose white flour*
- Sugar
- Brown Sugar
- Pasta—*Spaghetti, Macaroni, Penne, etc.*
- Breadcrumbs—*Plain and panko style*
- Cornstarch
- Honey
- Broth—*Beef, Chicken, Veggie, or you can keep bouillon cubes on hand if you prefer*

- Rice—*I love Jasmine rice*
- Peanut Butter
- Worcestershire Sauce
- Oils—*Olive oil, Canola Oil, Vegetable Oil and if you cook a lot of Asian recipes...Sesame Oil*
- Vinegars—*Apple Cider, White Wine, Red Wine, Rice Wine, Balsamic*
- Cooking Wines...or regular wine—*Red, White, Sherry*

REFRIGERATOR

At least once a week I am back at the grocery store stocking up on my refrigerator basics. These items have the shortest shelf life of all the basics, so make sure to buy the size that best fits your needs to reduce waste.

- Milk
- Eggs
- Butter
- Bacon—*thick cut or regular cut*

- Sour Cream or Plain Greek Yogurt
- Mayonnaise
- Mustard
- Ketchup

Since I'm always cooking and creating in my kitchen, I also always keep items like **fresh garlic, onions, limes, lemons and all sorts of fresh herbs (like cilantro and parsley) on hand**. Fresher is always better, but sometimes due to seasonal ingredients, dried herbs and spices will do the job. Now that you have a well-stocked kitchen, you're ready to tackle these simple and easy recipes like a champ!

CHAPTER ONE

LEAVE IT TO THE BIRDS
24 MOUTHWATERING POULTRY RECIPES

When it comes down to it, chicken is by far my favorite protein to work with. I love the versatility of it! From shredded chicken breast to grilled chicken burgers and anything in between, the possibilities to create easy meals are endless. It's that exact versatility that gives you the ability to easily transform 5 ingredients into 3 different meals.

Looking for the perfect meal to entertain during the summer months? You need to check out my Grilled Summer Platter (page 53), filled with grilled chicken, fresh grilled peaches and grilled brie topped with a homemade pesto. It's the perfect meal to bring friends and family together.

During the fall, warm up by bringing all the flavors of Thanksgiving to the table with my Thanksgiving Shepherd's Pie (page 58), or take "Taco Tuesday" to the next level with my Saucy Shredded Chicken Tacos (page 21)!

Chicken and turkey are great any time of the year, but I especially love buying when they go on sale. This cookbook isn't about budgeting meals, but chicken can definitely be a budget-friendly protein for larger families such as mine. That's why I always tend to "flock" toward the poultry section whenever I see a sale. So stock up and let me show you how to transform that bird into some tasty dinners your whole family will enjoy. There's something for everyone in this chapter, and I just know you're going to love it as much as I do!

CHEESY POTATO CRUSTED CHICKEN

I don't think I've ever seen my kids gobble up their dinner so fast as when I make this easy and tasty dish. I'm not sure if it's the cheesy hash browns, the moist and tender chicken, or the crispy bacon on top, but they go bonkers for it. Okay, I may go bonkers for it too.

YIELD: 4 SERVINGS

5 medium **red potatoes**

1 c (115 g) shredded **marbled cheddar**

2 tbsp (30 g) melted butter

1 tsp salt

1 tsp dried parsley

1 tsp garlic powder

½ tsp black pepper

4 boneless skinless **chicken breast** filets, pounded to an even thickness

Salt and pepper

4 strips **bacon**

3 c (217 g) **broccoli** florets, steamed till crisp-tender

Start by preheating your oven to 425°F (219°C), then bring a pot of lightly salted water to a boil. Scrub the potatoes until clean and carefully place them in the boiling water. Let them boil for 10 to 15 minutes, or until fork-tender, then run them under cold water until they've cooled and you're able to handle them. Use a cheese grater to shred the potatoes—some of the potato skins will get shredded but most fall away when shredding, so just discard those. Toss the shredded potatoes with the marbled cheddar, melted butter, salt, dried parsley, garlic powder and black pepper.

Season the chicken breasts with salt and pepper to taste, and place in a lightly greased baking dish. Divide the potato mixture into 4 equal parts and cover each chicken breast. Cut each strip of bacon into 2 pieces, and lay 2 pieces of bacon on each chicken breast.

Bake the chicken for 25 minutes or until the chicken is fully cooked and the bacon has crisped.

Serve it nice and hot with a side of steamed broccoli.

Shawn's Tip: Sometimes I like to turn the broiler on for the last couple of minutes to crisp up the top of the hash browns. Just be careful to not let it burn!

GRILLED CHICKEN WITH LOADED SMASHED POTATOES

This easy recipe is such a no-brainer, but I can't tell you how many times my husband has looked through the fridge and pantry and come to me saying that we have nothing to eat. I'll take a quick glace, see these key ingredients and *bam!* I've got dinner on the table in no time. I'm pretty sure he thinks I'm a magician.

YIELD: 4 SERVINGS

8 medium **red potatoes**
3 tbsp (45 ml) olive oil
Salt and pepper
1 c (115 g) **marbled cheddar**
½ c (120 g) cooked, crumbled **bacon**
4 boneless skinless **chicken breasts**
3 c (217 g) **broccoli** florets, steamed

Optional garnish: diced green onions and sour cream

Preheat the oven to 400°F (205°C).

Boil the potatoes in a pot of salted water until they become fork-tender, about 10 to 15 minutes. Drizzle half of the olive oil on a baking sheet and place the potatoes on, leaving room around them. Use a potato masher to flatten the potatoes to about ½ inch (1.3 cm) thickness. Brush the tops with olive oil and season with salt and pepper to taste. Bake for 20 minutes, then sprinkle the potatoes with the cheese and crumbled bacon. Return it to the oven for another 5 minutes to melt the cheese.

Meanwhile, pound the chicken breasts to an even thickness—a meat tenderizer or a sturdy rolling pin works great for this. Season the chicken with salt and pepper, then grill for 3 to 5 minutes per side on medium-high heat until the chicken reaches an internal temperature of 165°F (74°C). Then remove from the grill and loosely cover with foil for at least 5 minutes.

Serve the grilled chicken with the loaded smashed potatoes and steamed broccoli.

Shawn's Tip: I love to top my loaded smashed potatoes with a dollop of sour cream and a sprinkle of diced green onions. My husband loves my magic skills.

LOADED CHICKEN CASSEROLE

This casserole has been a long-standing family favorite in our house. It's always a fight to see who gets the last scoop! With tender chicken, roasted potatoes and broccoli all smothered in cheese and bacon bits, what's not to love about this simple and complete dinner!? We like to top it with sliced green onions, a dollop of sour cream and a few dashes of hot sauce for a little kick in the mouth!

YIELD: 6 SERVINGS

1 lb (455 g) boneless skinless **chicken breast**, cubed into 1-inch (2.5 cm) pieces

6 to 8 medium **red potatoes** cut into ½-inch (1.3 cm) pieces (or 3 c [540 g] of quartered baby red potatoes)

2 c (145 g) **broccoli** florets

¼ c (60 ml) olive oil

1 ½ tsp (8 g) salt

1 tbsp (7 g) paprika

2 tsp (7 g) garlic powder

2 c (230 g) shredded **marbled cheddar**

6 pieces **bacon**, cooked and crumbled

Optional garnish: sliced green onions, sour cream and hot sauce

Preheat the oven to 400°F (205°C). Spray a 9" x 13" (23 x 33 cm) casserole dish with cooking spray and set aside.

Combine the chicken, potatoes, broccoli, olive oil, salt, paprika and garlic powder in a large bowl. Toss to coat evenly. Pour into casserole dish. Bake for 55 to 60 minutes, stirring every 20 minutes, until the chicken is cooked through and the potatoes have slightly browned.

Remove from the oven and sprinkle with the marbled cheddar and crumbled bacon. Return to the oven for 5 minutes until the cheese is melted. Top with any optional garnishes you feel like!

Variation: This dish can easily be transformed into an Italian favorite by swapping out the paprika with equal amounts dried parsley and switching the marbled cheddar out with equal amounts mozzarella cheese.

SAUCY SHREDDED CHICKEN TACOS

Taco Tuesday? We don't discriminate in our house; tacos are eaten any day of the week!
These saucy chicken tacos are effortless yet packed full of flavor, which makes them a 5-star weeknight dinner.
Try pairing them with my spanish rice (on page 33) for a complete meal!

YIELD: 4 SERVINGS

2 c (280 g) shredded **rotisserie chicken**

1 c (150 g) grilled **corn kernels**, (drained canned corn kernels would work as well)

1 (15 oz [425 ml]) can **fire-roasted tomatoes**, drained

1 tsp chili powder

½ tsp cumin

½ tsp garlic powder

½ tsp onion powder

¼ tsp salt

8 **corn tortillas**

1 c (115 g) shredded **cheddar cheese**

Optional garnish: chopped lettuce, sour cream, chopped cilantro

Combine the chicken, corn, tomatoes, chili powder, cumin, garlic powder, onion powder and salt in a large skillet over medium heat. Stir until heated through. Warm the tortillas and keep warm until ready to serve.

Divide the chicken filling among the warm tortillas and top with the cheese and any additional toppings you desire.

Variation: These tacos also taste great with shredded beef or shredded pork.

EASY CHICKEN TORTILLA SOUP

My husband and I have this long-standing joke that you can create pretty much any Mexican dish with just meat, cheese and tortillas. We've traveled all over Mexico and have enjoyed many varieties of the combination. We can't get enough of the robust flavors in this simple soup, and it's become a staple in our house when the cooler weather starts to creep in.

YIELD: 6 SERVINGS

1 (15 oz [425 ml]) can **fire-roasted diced tomatoes**

1 tsp garlic powder

1 tsp onion powder

2 qt (8 c [2 L]) chicken broth

3 c (420 g) shredded **rotisserie chicken**

1 ½ c (225 g) grilled **corn kernels**, from about 2 ears of corn

1 tsp cumin

1 tsp chili powder

Salt and pepper

3 tsp (8 g) cornstarch, mixed with 1 tbsp (15 ml) water

4 corn and flour blend **tortillas**, cut into thin strips

1 ½ c (113 g) shredded **cheddar cheese**

Optional garnish: diced avocado, chopped cilantro

Blend the diced tomatoes, garlic and onion powder in a blender until smooth, then pour into a large Dutch oven and cook on medium-high heat until the liquid has reduced to half, about 5 minutes.

Stir in the chicken broth, chicken and corn, and then season with the cumin and chili powder. Taste the soup and then season with salt and pepper to taste.

Combine the 3 teaspoons (8 g) of cornstarch with 1 tablespoon (15 ml) of water and then stir into the soup. Bring the soup to a boil and then reduce the heat and simmer for 20 minutes, stirring occasionally.

Divide the tortilla strips among the serving bowls, ladle in the soup and top with cheese and any other optional garnish you desire.

Shawn's Tip: Bulk up this soup by using a Southwest blend of frozen vegetables that contains peppers, corn, onions, etc.

FIRE-ROASTED CHICKEN ENCHILADAS

When I lived in Canada, Mexican food was not something you saw very much of. In fact, buying things such as canned enchilada sauce wasn't even an option for me. I created my own recipe, and honestly, it's way better than the canned stuff! By using fire-roasted tomatoes as the base for these cheesy enchiladas along with grilled corn, this simple Mexican staple has a pop of flavor that you would not expect!

YIELD: 6 SERVINGS

1 (15 oz [425 ml]) can **fire-roasted diced tomatoes**

¼ c (60 ml) vegetable oil

2 tbsp (15 g) flour

1 tbsp (8 g) chili powder

1 c (240 ml) chicken broth

½ tsp cumin

½ tsp garlic salt

½ tsp onion powder

2 c (280 g) shredded **rotisserie chicken**, skin discarded

1 ear **corn**, grilled, kernels removed

2 c (230 g) **shredded cheddar cheese**

8 corn and flour blend **tortillas**

Optional garnish: chopped cilantro, sour cream

Preheat the oven to 350°F (177°C) and lightly coat a 9" x 13" (23 x 33 cm) casserole dish with nonstick cooking spray.

To make the enchilada sauce, place the diced tomatoes in a blender and process until smooth with no lumps, and set aside. In a large skillet, heat the vegetable oil over medium heat, then whisk in the flour and chili powder until it becomes smooth. Pour in the blended tomatoes and chicken broth along with the remaining spices, and whisk to combine. Let simmer until slightly thickened. Pour ½ cup (120 ml) of the sauce in the bottom of the casserole dish.

Meanwhile, combine the chicken with the grilled corn kernels and then place a heaping ¼ cup (35 g) on each tortilla along with a decent sprinkle of cheese. Roll each tortilla up and place seam-side down in the casserole dish. Cover with the remaining sauce and the rest of the cheese and bake for 20 to 25 minutes or until melted and bubbly all over.

Quick Tip: If you don't have time to make your own enchilada sauce, feel free to use the canned version.

Shawn's Notes: If you can't find the blended tortillas, regular corn tortillas will work in this recipe. Just be sure to heat them slightly before rolling so they do not break on you.

THAI CURRY CHICKEN PENNE

Unlike Indian curry, Thai curry is milder in flavor with a bit of heat from the Thai chilies used. The moist paste can be found in the Asian aisle of most grocery stores. The spice is usually tamed with the use of canned coconut milk, which also gives it a creamy and slightly nutty taste. I've combined my favorite Thai flavors in this quick and easy pasta dish that I love serving with extra chili garlic sauce on top for an extra kick of heat.

YIELD: 4 SERVINGS

2 c (210 g) uncooked **penne**

1 tbsp (15 ml) olive oil

1 lb (455 g) boneless skinless **chicken breast**, cut into 1 inch (2.5 cm) pieces

Salt and pepper

1 clove garlic, minced

2 tbsp (30 ml) red **Thai curry paste**

1 (13.5 oz [400 ml]) can **coconut milk**

1 c (135 g) frozen **peas**

Start by placing your uncooked penne in a large pot of lightly salted boiling water.

Meanwhile, heat the olive oil in a large skillet over medium heat. Season the chicken breast with salt and pepper and cook in the hot skillet, browning the chicken on all sides, until cooked through and no longer pink, about 5 to 7 minutes. Throw in the garlic and sauté with the chicken for 1 minute, then remove the chicken and garlic to a bowl and keep warm.

Return the skillet to the stovetop and add the Thai curry paste to the skillet, whisking for 30 seconds, until very fragrant. Gradually whisk in the coconut milk until fully combined, and then add the peas to the skillet and bring to a gentle boil. Reduce the heat to a simmer, add the chicken and its juices back to the pan and let simmer until the noodles are ready. Drain the noodles and then add them to the curry mixture, stirring to combine.

Shawn's Cooking Tip: If the sauce is too spicy, try adding a tablespoon (15 g) of brown sugar to balance out the heat. If you prefer the sauce spicier, whisk in an additional tablespoon (15 ml) of the Thai curry paste.

GRILLED THAI CHICKEN SKEWERS

Can we just agree that everything served on a stick is just that much better? I love making these chicken skewers because my kids can't get enough of them! The peas on the other hand, those have taken some getting acquainted with. Although, ever since I started growing our own peas in our garden, my kids have started enjoying them more and more. There's something about splitting open those fresh green peas that makes them that much more satisfying. Don't worry if you can't get ahold of fresh peas for this recipe, frozen works just as well!

YIELD: 4 SERVINGS

5 tbsp (75 ml) **red Thai curry paste**, divided

5 tbsp (75 ml) olive oil, divided + additional for coating the grill

2 lb (910 g) boneless skinless **chicken breasts** cut into 1 inch (2.5 cm) pieces

1 c (105 g) uncooked **penne noodles**

1 (13.5 oz [400 ml]) can **coconut milk**

2 tbsp (25 g) creamy peanut butter

¼ c (50 g) brown sugar

3 tbsp (45 ml) fresh lime juice

3 cloves garlic, minced

3 c (400 g) fresh or frozen **peas**, thawed

2 tbsp (30 g) butter

Salt and pepper

Wooden skewers

Optional garnish: chopped cilantro, lime wedges

Whisk together 4 tablespoons (60 ml) of the red Thai curry paste with 4 tablespoons (60 ml) of the olive oil and add the cut-up chicken pieces to the mixture. Let the mixture marinate for 2 to 4 hours. About 20 minutes before grilling, soak the wooden skewers in warm water to prevent burning.

Heat the grill over medium heat and brush it with olive oil to prevent sticking. Thread the chicken pieces onto the wooden skewers, and grill 3 to 4 minutes per side, until cooked through.

Meanwhile, cook the noodles according to package instructions, and prepare the sauce by combining the coconut milk and peanut butter in a small saucepan over medium-low heat. Whisk until smooth and then add the brown sugar and 1 tablespoon (15 ml) red Thai curry paste. Remove from the heat and whisk in the lime juice. Let the sauce cool and serve warm with the grilled chicken, and drizzle over the cooked penne noodles.

To prepare the peas, heat the remaining 1 tablespoon (15 ml) olive oil in a medium skillet over medium heat. Sauté the garlic for 30 to 45 seconds, until very fragrant, and then add the peas, sautéing until heated through, about 3 minutes. Remove from the heat and add the butter, and season with salt and pepper to taste.

> *Shawn's Tip:* Serve this dish platter-style, sprinkled with chopped cilantro and plenty of lime wedges on the side!

CRISPY THAI CHICKEN OVER BROWNED BUTTER PASTA

Have you unleashed the power of browned butter yet? It was just a few weeks before Thanksgiving several years ago when I was introduced to browned butter. I was at a foodie event, and we were taste-testing potential dishes to serve on turkey day. One dish required browned butter, and after one taste—let alone one whiff of the glorious aroma—I was hooked. The browned butter pasta has a nutty taste, which pairs wonderfully with the crispy pan-fried Thai chicken. Just use caution when making the browned butter because it can go from nutty and delicious to burnt and bitter real quick.

YIELD: 4 SERVINGS

4 boneless skinless **chicken breast** halves, pounded thin

¼ tsp salt

⅛ tsp black pepper

1 ½ tbsp (23 ml) **red Thai curry paste**

1 c (240 ml) **coconut milk**

2 c (210 g) uncooked **penne pasta**

1 c (135 g) frozen **peas**

¼ c (60 ml) canola oil

1 c (120 g) plain breadcrumbs

8 tbsp (113 g) butter

1 clove garlic, minced, optional

Season the chicken breast halves with salt and pepper, then whisk together the red Thai curry paste with the coconut milk in a shallow dish, and place the chicken in the mixture. Let the chicken marinate for at least 30 minutes, up to 2 hours.

Bring a large pot of lightly salted water to a boil and add the penne pasta. Cook according to package instructions, adding the peas to the boiling water just 3 minutes before finishing. Drain the pasta and peas and set aside.

Heat a skillet over medium heat and add the canola oil. Remove the chicken from the coconut milk mixture, letting any excess drip off, dip the chicken in breadcrumbs to coat, and then carefully place in the hot skillet. Cook for 2 to 3 minutes per side, until golden brown.

Meanwhile in another large skillet, heat the butter over medium heat, stirring occasionally until the butter begins to foam slightly. Swirl the pan gently every few seconds until the butter begins to gain a light brown color and releases a nutty aroma. Toss in the pasta and peas and remove from the heat. Serve the crispy chicken over the hot pasta.

Shawn's Tip: Add 1 clove of minced garlic to the browned butter for an extra burst of flavor.

FIESTA STUFFED CHICKEN

There's a party going on inside this chicken! The delicious filling is loaded with cheese, black beans, salsa and spices. I give the chicken a good sear in a cast iron skillet before finishing the cooking process inside the oven. This helps to boost the flavor and increase the moisture of the chicken.

YIELD: 4 SERVINGS

4 boneless skinless **chicken breasts**

½ c (80 g) **black beans,** rinsed and drained

½ c (60 g) **cheddar cheese**, grated

3 tbsp (45 ml) **salsa**

¼ tsp salt

¼ tsp garlic powder

¼ tsp chili powder

¼ tsp cumin

2 tbsp (5 g) fresh chopped cilantro, optional

1 tbsp (15 ml) olive oil

Salt and pepper

FOR THE SPANISH RICE

2 tsp (10 ml) olive oil

1 c (160 g) uncooked long grain white **rice**

½ tsp garlic salt

½ tsp cumin

1 ½ c (355 ml) **salsa**

1 ½ c (355 ml) chicken broth

Preheat the oven to 350°F (177°C).

Use a sharp knife to make an incision in the side of each chicken breast to make a pocket for the filling. Combine the black beans, cheese, salsa, salt, garlic powder, chili powder, cumin and optional fresh cilantro in a small bowl, and then stuff each chicken breast with the mixture. Use a toothpick to secure it closed.

Heat a cast iron skillet (or a heavy oven-safe skillet) over medium-high heat and add the olive oil to the pan, swirling it around to coat. Season the chicken breasts with salt and pepper, then place top side down in the skillet and sear for 2 minutes to get a nice color to it, then carefully flip and sear the other side for an additional 4 minutes. Place the skillet in the oven and cook for an additional 20 minutes, or until the chicken is cooked through.

Meanwhile, make the Spanish rice by heating the olive oil in a large pan over medium heat. Add the rice and lightly toast it for about 2 minutes. Then stir in the garlic salt, cumin, salsa and chicken broth. Bring the mixture to a boil, and then reduce the heat to low and cover with a lid. Let the rice cook for 18 to 20 minutes, fluff with a fork and serve with your Fiesta Stuffed Chicken.

Shawn's Tip: If you don't have a cast iron or oven-safe skillet, you can sear the chicken in a regular skillet and then place the chicken breasts in a casserole dish to finish cooking in the oven.

CHICKEN AND BLACK BEAN BURGERS

These tasty chicken burgers have cheese and spices throughout, which gives them crispy edges and tender, flavorful insides. Top these saucy burgers with a few slices of avocado, and you'll never look at a chicken burger the same way again!

YIELD: 6 SERVINGS

1 lb (455 g) ground **chicken**

½ c (80 g) **black beans**, drained and lightly mashed

½ c (80 g) cooked white **rice**, cooled

1 tsp chili powder

½ tsp garlic powder

½ tsp cumin

½ tsp onion powder

½ tsp salt

1 egg, lightly beaten

½ c (60 g) **cheddar cheese**, grated

Salt and pepper

6 hamburger buns, optional

6 (1 oz [28 g]) **cheddar cheese** slices

½ c (120 ml) **salsa**

Optional garnish: sliced avocado

In a large bowl, gently combine the ground chicken, black beans, rice, all the spices, egg and grated cheddar cheese. Use your hands to get in there and give it a good mix. Form the chicken mixture into 6 equal-size patties and season with salt and pepper on each side. Grill the patties over medium heat for 3 to 4 minutes per side, or until the center is no longer pink. Let the burgers rest under a sheet of tinfoil until ready to serve.

Place each cooked patty on a toasted hamburger bun with a slice of cheddar cheese and a tablespoon (15 ml) of salsa!

Side Note: I love using my meat grinder to turn chicken breasts into ground chicken. If you don't have a meat grinder, just ask your grocery store butcher to grind the chicken for you!

SLOW COOKER
SALSA CHICKEN RICE BOWLS

Chicken is marinated all day in your favorite salsa till it practically falls apart and becomes super tender.
This chicken is great wrapped up in tortillas, on top of a salad, or my personal favorite—over a bed of rice!

YIELD: 4 SERVINGS

4 boneless skinless **chicken breasts**
Salt and pepper
1 ½ c (355 ml) **salsa**
1 c (160 g) **black beans**, drained
1 c (160 g) white or brown **rice**
1 c (120 g) **cheddar cheese**, grated

Optional additions: 1 c (140 g) frozen corn kernels, chopped fresh cilantro and a dollop of sour cream

Season the chicken with salt and pepper and place at the bottom of your slow cooker. Pour the salsa and black beans over top, then cook on low for 6 to 8 hours, or on high for 3 to 4 hours.

Just before serving prepare the rice according to the package instructions, and use two forks to pull apart and shred the chicken. It should fall apart pretty easily. Serve on top of the white or brown rice with a sprinkle of cheddar cheese on top.

Shawn's Tip: Add some extra color to the dish by throwing in a cup (140 g) of frozen corn kernels before cooking, then garnish with a little bit of chopped cilantro and a dollop of sour cream!

BROILED ASIAN CHICKEN THIGHS WITH RED PEPPER SLAW

I love this quick and easy dinner recipe. The chicken thighs are quickly seared in the pan, and then finished off under the broiler, where they are basted in the most delicious Asian–inspired sauce. Cut your peppers and onions really thin and let them soak up the sweet and tangy orange vinaigrette while the chicken cooks.

YIELD: 4 SERVINGS

1 tbsp (15 ml) **orange marmalade**

2 tbsp (30 ml) apple cider vinegar

2 tbsp (30 ml) olive oil, divided

Dash of red pepper flakes

Salt and pepper

1 **red bell pepper**, very thinly sliced

1 c (130 g) **purple onion**, very thinly sliced

4 boneless, skin-on **chicken thighs**, pounded to an even thickness, *see cooking tip for directions*

2 tbsp (30 g) butter, melted

2 tbsp (30 ml) **soy sauce**

1 tsp garlic powder

½ tsp dried parsley

⅛ tsp black pepper

Optional garnish: freshly chopped cilantro

Turn on the oven's broiler to high.

Whisk together the orange marmalade, apple cider vinegar, 1 tablespoon (15 ml) olive oil and red pepper flakes in a large bowl, then season with salt and pepper to taste. Toss in the thinly sliced pepper and onion, and set in the fridge until ready to serve.

Meanwhile, heat the remaining 1 tablespoon (15 ml) of oil in an oven-safe skillet over medium-high heat. Season the chicken thighs with salt and pepper, then sear the chicken, skin-side first, for 2 minutes. Flip and cook for an additional 2 minutes. Combine the butter, soy sauce, garlic powder, dried parsley and black pepper in a small bowl, and brush each chicken thigh with the mixture, reserving some for later. Place the skillet in the oven, about 5 inches (13 cm) from the broiler, and cook an additional 3 to 5 minutes or until skin is browned and crispy. Baste with a little more sauce if desired.

Serve with a side of the tangy red pepper slaw, and garnish with freshly chopped cilantro, if desired.

Variation: Try adding thinly sliced cabbage and carrots to the slaw to bulk up on the veggies.

Shawn's Cooking Tip: Don't be afraid of deboning a chicken thigh, it is actually really easy! Lay it skin side down on a cutting board. Using the tip of the knife, score a line through the meat along the length of the bone. Expose the bone and then carefully slide the knife underneath the bone, so the blade is perpendicular to the bone and facing away from you. Grasp the chicken thigh behind the knife with your non-knife hand and slide the blade away from you, underneath the bone until it pops out the other side. Turn the chicken thigh around and repeat the process, fully removing the bone from the thigh.

ORANGE CHICKEN STIR-FRY

Stir-fries are great for using up any extra veggies you have hanging around in your fridge. The key is to not overcook them, but to give them a good quick sear and leave a little bite to them. The sauce always goes in last to bring it all together, and then serve it over a bed of hot rice.

YIELD: 4 SERVINGS

⅓ c (80 ml) chicken broth

⅓ c (80 ml) **orange marmalade**

2 tbsp (30 ml) **soy sauce**

½ tsp garlic powder

Pinch of red pepper flakes

2 tbsp (30 ml) olive oil, divided

1 **red bell pepper**, coarsely chopped

½ **purple onion**, coarsely chopped

1 lb (455 g) **chicken thighs**, boneless, skinless, cut into bite-size pieces

¼ c (35 g) cornstarch

Optional garnish: sliced green onions

Combine the chicken broth, orange marmalade, soy sauce, garlic powder and red pepper flakes in a small bowl, then whisk to combine. Set this aside for later.

Heat a wok or large skillet over medium-high heat. Add 1 tablespoon (15 ml) of oil to the pan and cook the peppers and onions for 2 to 3 minutes, stirring frequently. Remove the pepper and onion from the pan and set aside.

Heat the remaining tablespoon (15 ml) of oil in the wok or skillet and toss the bite-size pieces of chicken in the cornstarch, shaking off any excess. Add the chicken to the pan, being careful not to overcrowd the pan. You may have to do this in a couple batches. Brown the chicken on all sides, about 2 to 3 minutes per batch. Once all the chicken is cooked, add the vegetables back to the pan, then stir in the sauce and heat it through until it bubbles and thickens. Garnish with sliced green onions if desired.

Shawn's Tip: If you like your sauce thicker, make a quick slurry by combining 1 teaspoon of cornstarch with 1 tablespoon (15 ml) of water, then pour it into the sauce in your pan and stir. Let it bubble, and it will begin to thicken.

Variation: Boneless, skinless chicken breast can be used to substitute for the chicken thighs.

HAWAIIAN CHICKEN SKEWERS

Hands down, this is one of my favorite ways to enjoy grilled chicken. Who can resist food served on a stick? Especially when it's a delicious chicken that has been marinated in a sweet Hawaiian–inspired sauce with a little hint of orange marmalade. You might want to double this recipe, because this chicken goes fast!

YIELD: 4 TO 6 SERVINGS

8 boneless, skinless **chicken thighs**

½ c (120 ml) chicken broth (or substitute with optional ½ c [120 ml] pineapple juice)

3 tbsp (45 ml) **orange marmalade**

1 c (240 ml) **soy sauce**

½ tsp ground ginger

½ tsp garlic powder

16 wooden skewers

1 **purple onion**, cut into 1-inch (2.5 cm) pieces

1 **red bell pepper**, cut into 1-inch (2.5 cm) pieces

Olive oil

Optional, for serving: white or brown rice

In a large zip-top bag, combine the chicken thighs, chicken broth, orange marmalade, soy sauce, ginger and garlic powder. Gently squish the mixture around until combined, and let it marinate in the fridge for 2 to 4 hours.

Before grilling, soak your wooden skewers in water for at least 20 minutes so they do not burn on the grill.

Thread your chicken thighs onto the wooden skewers. With the onion and pepper pieces, make skewers of vegetables, and then spritz them with a little olive oil or cooking spray. Heat the grill and then brush with olive oil to prevent any sticking. Grill the chicken and vegetables over medium heat until the chicken is cooked through and the vegetables have charred slightly. Enjoy over some cooked rice if desired.

Variation: This recipe would also work great with chicken breast tenders, just make sure to pound the chicken to an even thickness and then skewer onto sticks!

GRILLED BALSAMIC CHICKEN WITH ROASTED SUMMER VEGETABLES

When I planted 12 tomato plants, I thought surely my black thumb would kill all but one. Surprisingly all 12 survived and flourished. I quickly learned all the ways to eat a tomato. Roasting grape or cherry tomatoes is a fantastic way to release their sweet flavor and bring so much more dimension to a dish.

YIELD: 4 SERVINGS

1 large **zucchini**, sliced into sticks

1 large **onion**, quartered

1 c (150 g) whole grape or cherry **tomatoes**

2 tbsp (30 ml) olive oil, divided

Salt and pepper

½ c (70 g) **mozzarella cheese**, cubed

4 boneless skinless **chicken breasts**

2 tsp (10 ml) balsamic vinegar

Heat the grill to medium heat and preheat the oven to 425°F (219°C).

Combine all the zucchini sticks, onion quarters and tomatoes in a bowl. Add 1 tablespoon (15 ml) of olive oil, salt and pepper to taste, and then toss to combine. Spread out on a rimmed baking sheet, and roast in the oven for 15 to 20 minutes, stirring halfway. Vegetables should be lightly charred, and the tomato skins will blister and crack. Once the vegetables are done cooking, remove from the oven, toss in the mozzarella cubes and let them soften and melt slightly.

Meanwhile, season the chicken breasts with salt and pepper. Drizzle with just a little bit of olive oil, then grill for 4 to 6 minutes per side, or until cooked through. Before taking the chicken off the grill, brush each breast with a little balsamic vinegar, then serve with the roasted vegetables.

Shawn's Grilling Tip: For the BEST grilled chicken, place the chicken breasts between two sheets of parchment paper, and use a heavy object like a rolling pin to pound the chicken to an even thickness. After it's grilled, place it on a plate and cover it loosely with foil to rest for at least 5 minutes. Using these methods will result in a juicier chicken breast every time!

CARAMELIZED ONION CHICKEN DINNER

Cheesy chicken and caramelized onions, all on top of a bed of zucchini! These foil dinners
are one of the first recipes I created for my husband and me when we were just barely newlyweds.
My favorite part is how easy the cleanup is!

YIELD: 4 SERVINGS

1 large **zucchini**, sliced into
½ inch (1.27 cm) disks
Salt and pepper
4 boneless skinless **chicken breasts**
4 oz (115 g) **mozzarella cheese**, sliced
1 tbsp (15 g) butter
1 large **onion**, sliced
½ c (80 g) diced **tomatoes**

Heat oven to 375°F (191°C).

Lightly coat 4 (12"-long [31 cm]) sheets of aluminum foil with cooking spray. Place a quarter of the zucchini slices in the center of each sheet of foil, then season with salt and pepper to taste. Season each chicken breast with salt and pepper as well. Take a sharp knife and make three incisions on the top of each chicken breast at a 45 degree angle, about 1 inch (2.5 cm) apart. Place a slice of mozzarella cheese in each incision, then place the chicken breast on top of the zucchini slices.

Heat the butter in a pan over medium-high heat. Add the sliced onion, and sauté until the onion slices have turned golden brown, about 10 minutes. Top each chicken breast with a quarter of the onions. Seal up the foil pouches by bringing the longer ends of the foil together and folding several times over, then pinch together the smaller open ends and roll up to seal.

Place the pouches on a baking sheet and bake for 20 to 25 minutes—longer if your chicken breasts were thicker—until the chicken breasts are fully cooked. Carefully unwrap the foil, drain any excess juices from the pouch and then top with the diced tomatoes.

> *Variation:* Try switching out the zucchini for fresh green beans or yellow summer squash.

CHICKEN MILANESE WITH ZUCCHINI NOODLES

Zucchini noodles are all the rage these days. By using just a simple box grater, you can whip up some healthy green noodles in no time! Top those green strings with some roasted tomato sauce and a quick fast-fried breaded chicken breast, and it's a complete meal your whole family will enjoy!

YIELD: 4 SERVINGS

4 tsp plus 1 tbsp (35 ml) olive oil, divided

16 **Roma tomatoes**, halved and seeds removed

1 medium **onion**, quartered

2 tsp (10 g) Italian seasoning

1 tsp garlic powder

1 tbsp (15 g) sugar

1 tsp salt

½ tsp black pepper

4 boneless, skinless **chicken breasts**

Salt and pepper

1 egg, lightly beaten

1 c (120 g) Italian breadcrumbs, or plain breadcrumbs seasoned with 1 tsp Italian seasoning

4 (1 oz [28 g]) slices **mozzarella cheese**

3 large **zucchini**

1 tbsp (15 g) butter

Preheat the oven to 415°F (213°C). Line a rimmed baking sheet with foil and then drizzle with 2 teaspoons (10 ml) olive oil.

In a large bowl, combine the halved tomatoes, onion, Italian seasoning, garlic powder, sugar, salt and pepper and another 2 teaspoons (10 ml) olive oil. Stir to coat evenly, then pour on the baking sheet and place in the oven for 25 to 30 minutes, stirring the mixture halfway through. You'll know it's done when the tomatoes have blistered and have started to caramelize.

Carefully pour the tomatoes into a blender and remove the center of the lid to vent. Cover the hole with a clean cloth and blend the tomatoes until they become a thick sauce. Set this aside and start working on your chicken.

Place the chicken breasts between two sheets of parchment paper and use a rolling pin or heavy pan to pound the chicken into a thin, even layer. Season with salt and pepper, dip them into the egg, letting any excess drip off, then coat with the breadcrumbs.

Heat an oven-safe skillet over medium heat, and add 1 tablespoon (15 ml) of olive oil to the pan. Cook the chicken for 2 to 3 minutes per side, and then spread 2 tablespoons (30 ml) of the tomato sauce on each chicken breast and top with the mozzarella cheese. Place under the broiler for a minute or two to melt the cheese.

Meanwhile, use the large grate of your cheese grater to make long passes with your zucchini to make zucchini noodles. Keep slicing until you reach the core of the zucchini where the seeds are and then stop. Save the cores for another use, such as thickening soups, adding to stir fries, etc.

Melt the butter in a saucepan over medium heat, toss in the zucchini noodles and stir until heated through and tender. Season with salt and pepper and serve immediately with extra tomato sauce and the cheese topped chicken breast on the side.

Shawn's Quick Tip: If you're short on time, skip the homemade sauce and just use tomato slices or jarred tomato sauce to top the chicken breasts before adding the mozzarella cheese.

PEACH STUFFED CHICKEN ROLLS

I have a weakness for soft cheeses. Brie is one of those soft cheeses. I have fond memories of girls' nights huddled around a warm fire, watching *Downton Abbey* and devouring several wheels of cheese, while laughing and enjoying ourselves. I love the fact that I've stuck all that yummy creamy goodness inside of a chicken breast and brightened it up with some fresh peaches and fresh basil. I've even thrown in some toasted pine nuts for some added texture and a delightful nutty flavor. Basically, this chicken will bring a smile to your face.

YIELD: 4 SERVINGS

4 boneless skinless **chicken breasts**
Salt and pepper
½ c (15 g) fresh **basil leaves**
1 ripe **peach,** pitted and diced
2 tbsp (20 g) toasted **pine nuts**
4 thick slices of **Brie cheese**
1 tbsp (15 ml) olive oil

Preheat the oven to 375°F (191°C).

Using a sharp knife, carefully butterfly your chicken breasts, opening them up like a page in a book. Place the chicken breasts between two sheets of parchment paper and pound them to an even thickness. Season the chicken with salt and pepper.

Lay a few fresh basil leaves on one side of each chicken breast, top with a tablespoon (10 g) of diced peaches and ½ tablespoon (5 g) of pine nuts. Lay 1 slice of Brie on top of that and fold the chicken over the filling, using a toothpick to secure it closed.

Heat the olive oil in a large oven-safe skillet—I use my cast iron skillet—and sear the chicken for 3 minutes per side, then transfer the skillet to the oven for an additional 10 to 15 minutes, or until cooked through. The Brie might ooze out a bit around the chicken, just scoop it up and serve with the cooked chicken. This chicken pairs perfectly with a simple side salad.

Variation: Switch up the fresh filling by using diced pears, toasted walnuts and blue cheese, along with the fresh basil, for a tasty twist!

GRILLED SUMMER PLATTER

The first house my husband and I bought was in a small town in southern Utah. The house was tiny, and the backyard wasn't more than a strip of grass with a giant peach tree in one corner and a grape vine in the other. That first summer, we were blown away by the amount of peaches that one tree produced. We were giving away peaches by the bucket, and still had so many peaches that I soon became the "Bubba Gump" of the peach world. If you've never grilled a peach before, you're in for a sweet treat. And *puh-lease*, grilled Brie is just a no-brainer. Grab a cedar plank to grill the cheese on though; otherwise you'll end up with a gooey mess in your grill.

YIELD: 4 SERVINGS

1 cedar plank—you can find these near the seafood section of your grocery store

4 boneless skinless **chicken breasts**, pounded to an even thickness

3 tbsp (45 ml) olive oil, divided

Salt and pepper

1 tsp fresh **basil**, chopped

4 ripe **peaches**, halved and pits removed

1 wheel of **Brie cheese**

FOR THE PESTO SAUCE

2 cloves garlic

2 c (50 g) **fresh basil**

¼ c (35 g) **pine nuts**

½ c (120 ml) olive oil

1 tsp salt

Soak a cedar plank in warm water for 10 minutes. Heat the grill over medium-high heat and brush with olive oil to prevent sticking.

Brush the chicken breasts with 1 tablespoon (15 ml) olive oil, and season both sides with salt and pepper.

In a small dish, whisk together 2 tablespoons (30 ml) olive oil with the chopped basil, salt and pepper to taste. Brush the flesh sides of the peaches with the basil-olive oil mixture.

Unwrap the Brie cheese, place on top of the cedar plank and place on the grill for 6 to 8 minutes or until it's softened.

Grill the chicken for 3 to 4 minutes per side, until cooked through. Grill the peaches, flesh side down, beside the chicken for 2 to 4 minutes, until grill marks have formed.

Meanwhile, prepare the pesto sauce by adding the 2 cloves of garlic to a food processor and pulsing it a few times until finely chopped. Add the basil and pine nuts and process until combined. With the food processor running, slowly drizzle the olive oil in through the chute until smooth. Season with the salt, and pulse a few more times. Serve the pesto on top of the warm Brie and alongside the grilled chicken and peaches.

Shawn's Tip: Add another dimension of flavor to the pesto sauce by toasting the pine nuts beforehand. Start by heating a dry skillet over medium heat, then add the pine nuts to the hot pan, shaking the pan every 10 seconds until the pine nuts turn a golden brown. Let them cool completely before adding to the pesto sauce.

BASIL PEACH CHICKEN SKILLET

I used to not be a fan of warm fruits with savory dishes, but I'm starting to feel like the sweet bursts from fresh fruit have so much to offer. The peaches in this quick chicken skillet give it a brightness that marries well with the aromatic basil. The sweet and savory flavors of this dish are fantastic over a bed of quinoa, couscous or even rice, which helps to soak up all that delicious sauce.

YIELD: 4 SERVINGS

4 boneless skinless **chicken breasts,** cut into 1-inch (2.5 cm) pieces

Salt and pepper

1 tbsp (15 ml) olive oil

1 shallot, thinly sliced

2 cloves garlic, minced

1 c (240 ml) chicken broth

10 fresh **basil** leaves, sliced into ribbons + 4 more leaves

⅓ c (50 g) Brie

3 large **peaches**, peeled and cut into thin slices

¼ c (35 g) toasted **pine nuts** (see pg 53 for toasting directions)

Optional garnish: fresh basil

Optional, for serving: quinoa, couscous or rice

Season the chicken breast pieces with salt and pepper.

Heat the olive oil in a large skillet and cook the chicken for 2 to 3 minutes per side, until browned and cooked through, tossing in the shallot and garlic in the last 2 minutes, to soften and become fragrant. Remove the chicken from the skillet and keep warm.

Return the skillet to the stovetop and add the chicken broth, using a wooden spoon to break up any browned bits on the bottom of the pan. Stir in the 10 sliced basil leaves, brie and peaches. Cook until the mixture reduces and thickens slightly, about 6 minutes. Return the chicken to the skillet and toss with the peach sauce. Serve the chicken over cooked quinoa, couscous or rice and top with 4 fresh basil leaves and toasted pine nuts.

Shawn's Tip: Since basil is so delicate to work with, you want to make as few cuts as possible without damaging the leaf. In order to make perfect ribbons of basil, stack your leaves on top of each other and tightly roll them up. Use a sharp knife to make small cuts starting at one end of the roll and work your way down.

MINI CHEESE-STUFFED TURKEY MEATLOAVES WITH MUSHROOM GRAVY

The trick to making a good turkey meatloaf is to keep it moist and tender. How do you do that? Mushrooms! Finely diced mushrooms add moisture to these cute mini meatloaves; top them with the quick mushroom gravy, and it's irresistible! I'm also swooning over these stovetop roasted sweet potatoes with green beans, which add so much color and flavor, making this a complete home-cooked classic you'll return to over and over again.

YIELD: 4 SERVINGS

1 c (75 g) finely diced **mushrooms**

1 tbsp (15 g) butter

1 lb (455 g) **ground turkey**

1 egg

½ tsp garlic powder

½ tsp onion powder

1 tsp Italian seasoning

½ c (60 g) plain breadcrumbs

Salt and pepper

4 tsp (20 g) **gournay cheese spread**, such as Boursin Garlic and Fine Herbs

2 tbsp (30 ml) olive oil

1 large **sweet potato**, peeled and diced into bite-size pieces

2 c (200 g) trimmed and cut fresh **green beans**

FOR THE MUSHROOM GRAVY

2 c (150 g) sliced **mushrooms**

2 tbsp (30 g) butter

1 c (240 ml) chicken broth

1 tbsp (8 g) cornstarch

1 tbsp (15 ml) water

Salt and pepper

Preheat the oven to 425°F (219°C). Line a baking sheet with foil, place an oven-safe rack on top and spritz with nonstick spray, then set aside.

Sauté the mushrooms in the butter until they turn soft, about 2 to 3 minutes, then place them in a large bowl. Add the ground turkey, egg, garlic powder, onion powder, Italian seasoning, breadcrumbs and salt and pepper to the bowl. Use your hands to incorporate all the ingredients together, and then divide the mixture into 4 small loaves shaped like mini footballs.

Use your finger to poke a hole in the center of each meatloaf, but not all the way through. Stuff a teaspoon of the gournay cheese inside each hole, then close the hole by pinching the meat around it. Place on the rack and bake for 25 minutes, or until the internal temperature reaches 165°F (74°C).

In a large pan with a lid, heat the olive oil over medium-high heat. Toss in the diced sweet potatoes and let cook, shaking the pan a few times per minute, until the sweet potatoes have lightly browned. Toss in the green beans and cover, shaking the pan every once in a while until the green beans and sweet potatoes are tender, about 5 to 7 minutes.

To make the mushroom gravy, sauté the mushrooms in the butter until soft, about 5 minutes, then add the the chicken broth and bring to a light boil. Combine the cornstarch and water and pour into the mushroom gravy, stirring until it begins to thicken. Season with salt and pepper to taste, and serve over the mini meatloaves.

Shawn's Quick Tip: Look for the pre-sliced mushroom blends at the grocery store to save yourself time on prep.

Variation: This recipe would also work great with ground beef in place of the ground turkey; just look for a leaner ground beef.

THANKSGIVING SHEPHERD'S PIE

Everything you love about Thanksgiving, shoved straight into this easy and quick casserole! Ground turkey, sliced mushrooms and fresh cut green beans are swimming in a creamy gravy, then topped with a layer of fluffy mashed sweet potatoes. The only thing missing is your Auntie pinching your cheeks and telling you how big you've grown.

YIELD: 4 SERVINGS

3 large **sweet potatoes**, peeled and cubed

½ c (120 ml) milk

5 tbsp (70 g) butter, divided

1 tsp garlic powder

Salt and pepper

1 lb (455 g) **ground turkey**

1 ½ c (112 g) sliced **mushrooms**

1 c (100 g) fresh **green beans**, trimmed and cut

2 tbsp (15 g) flour

1 c (240 ml) chicken broth

2 tsp (10 ml) Worcestershire sauce

4 tbsp (60 g) **gournay cheese spread**, such as Boursin Garlic and Fine Herbs

Optional garnish: fresh chopped parsley

Preheat the oven to 375°F (191°C). Lightly spray a 9" x 9" (23 x 23 cm) casserole dish with nonstick spray, and set aside.

Place the sweet potatoes in a large pot and cover with water. Boil until the potatoes are tender, then drain and return to the pot. Add the milk, 3 tablespoons (42 g) butter, garlic powder, salt and pepper, and mash until smooth and creamy, then set aside.

Meanwhile, brown the ground turkey in a pan, using a spoon to break up and crumble. Add the mushrooms and green beans to the pan, stirring occasionally for 5 minutes.

In a separate small pan, make a simple roux by melting the remaining 2 tablespoons (28 g) of butter, then whisking in the flour until smooth. Gradually pour in the chicken broth, still whisking to prevent any lumps. Add the Worcestershire sauce and the gournay cheese, whisking until smooth, creamy and thickened. Pour into the ground turkey mixture, stir to combine and transfer to the casserole dish. Top with the mashed sweet potatoes, and bake for 25 to 30 minutes or until bubbly all around. Garnish with fresh chopped parsley if desired.

Shawn's Quick Tip: If you don't have time to make the gravy, you can substitute 1 ½ cups (355 ml) of store-bought chicken gravy. Just blend in the gournay cheese before adding it to the ground turkey mixture.

ARTISAN TURKEY BURGERS WITH SWEET AND SPICY SWEET POTATO FRIES

My husband's job requires him to travel a lot so for about 10 months, we decided to take our family on the road and travel with him. We stayed in our 5th wheel trailer at several campsites all over the country, grilling nearly every single night. Turkey burgers became our favorite meal, and we topped them with all sorts of delicious things. Sautéed mushrooms with creamy cheeses were one of our favorites. Let's not get into my serious weakness for sweet potato fries...

YIELD: 4 SERVINGS

FOR THE SWEET POTATO FRIES

2 large **sweet potatoes**

¼ c (60 ml) extra virgin olive oil

1 tsp salt

1 tsp sugar

¼ tsp cinnamon

⅛ tsp cayenne pepper

FOR THE TURKEY BURGERS

1 lb (455 g) **ground turkey**

¼ c (30 g) plain breadcrumbs

2 tbsp (30 g) mayo

1 tsp Italian seasoning

¼ tsp garlic powder

Salt and pepper

1 tbsp (15 g) butter

1 c (75 g) sliced **mushrooms**

4 tbsp (60 g) crumbled **gournay cheese**, such as Boursin Garlic and Fine Herbs

4 hamburger buns, optional

Optional toppings: lettuce, sliced tomato, sliced purple onion

To make the sweet potato fries, preheat the oven to 450°F (233°C).

Wash the sweet potatoes and dry completely. Cut off the pointy ends of the sweet potato and slice them in half length-wise and into thin, even fries. Place in a bowl and toss with the remaining ingredients to coat. Place in an even layer on a baking sheet and bake for 25 minutes, flipping halfway. Serve hot with the turkey burgers!

To make the turkey burgers, heat the grill to medium heat and brush the grates with olive oil.

Combine the ground turkey, breadcrumbs, mayo, Italian seasoning and garlic powder in a large bowl, season with salt and pepper, and use your hands to incorporate into 4 equal patties. Season each side of the patties with salt and pepper, then grill for 3 to 4 minutes per side, or until cooked through.

Meanwhile, melt the butter over medium heat and sauté the sliced mushrooms until soft and tender, about 5 minutes. Top each burger with a tablespoon (15 g) of crumbled gournay cheese and some sautéed mushrooms. Serve each burger on a hamburger bun with a side of sweet potato fries.

Shawn's Tip: If you don't want to heat up the grill outside, try using a castiron grill pan on the stovetop. Just make sure to brush with olive oil before using to prevent any sticking.

CHAPTER TWO

MEAT ME IN THE KITCHEN
24 THICK AND JUICY MEAT RECIPES

Being a food blogger has given me a newfound love for food, especially when it comes to knowing where that food came from. A few years ago, I had the opportunity to go to a cattle ranch and learn all about beef. I've always loved a good steak, and let's face it, ground beef is a staple in my freezer, but now I truly appreciate all the different cuts of beef, as well as the nutritional value they bring to my meals.

Drift off to the Mediterranean with my Pan Seared Greek Steaks and Spanakopita Stuffed Tomatoes (page 96), or take it easy with my Mom's favorite, one-skillet Roasted Steak and Root Vegetables (page 100). If you're in a real pinch for time, you need to try my super quick BBQ Pulled Pork Flautas (page 72); they're always a favorite in my house!

From ground beef to pulled pork, this chapter is full of delicious recipes that you and your family can enjoy over and over again!

A FEW TIPS WHEN IT COMES TO STEAK:
• Internal temperature for steaks–Medium Rare: 145°F (63°C); Medium: 160°F (72°C); Well Done: 170°F (77°C).

• Let your steaks rest for at least 5 minutes after cooking before cutting in to them.

• Always cut against the grain to achieve a tender bite.

SLOW COOKER BALSAMIC GLAZED PULLED PORK

I dare you to stop after just one bite of this tender pulled pork. It's impossible. I have an obsession with this pulled pork; it's sweet, it's savory, it's tender, it's irresistible. This pork is the perfect jumping point for several easy dinners, but our favorite is when it's served hot inside a toasted ciabatta bun and topped with a generous helping of cool and creamy Brussels Sprout and Apple Slaw (page 76). Go ahead, I dare you.

YIELD: 4 SERVINGS

2 ½ lb (1 kg) **pork tenderloin**
Salt and pepper
1 c (240 ml) water, divided
1 **onion**, diced
1 tsp garlic powder
1 c (200 g) **brown sugar**
2 tbsp (15 g) cornstarch
½ c (120 ml) **balsamic vinegar**
4 tbsp (60 ml) **soy sauce**

Optional, for serving: ciabatta bun and Brussels Sprout and Apple Slaw (p 76)

Season the pork tenderloin with salt and pepper, then fill the slow cooker with ½ cup (120 ml) of water along with the pork and diced onion. Cook on low for 6 to 8 hours, and in the last hour of cooking, start working on the glaze.

To make the glaze, heat a small pot over medium-high heat and add the remaining ½ cup (120 ml) of water, garlic powder, brown sugar, cornstarch, balsamic vinegar and soy sauce. Bring the mixture to a boil, then reduce the heat and let simmer until the glaze has thickened, about 5 minutes. Brush the tops of the tenderloins with the glaze every 20 minutes for the last hour of cooking.

Remove the tenderloin from the slow cooker and place on a baking sheet. Brush the tenderloins again with the glaze and then place under the broiler for 2 to 3 minutes to give it a nice sweet and sticky texture. The pork should just fall apart when shredded with two forks. Use the leftover glaze to serve with the pulled pork.

Shawn's Cooking Tip: Since pork tenderloin is not a fatty cut of pork, I find the best way to get an ultra-tender pulled pork is to cook it low and slow. While you can cook this on high for 3 to 4 hours, I find that it's at peak tenderness when cooked on low for the full 8 hours.

BACON WRAPPED PORK TENDERLOIN

I'm going to go out on a limb here and assume that you're like me and have at least 3 pounds of bacon in your fridge at all times. *No?* Maybe that's a little extreme, but my husband is an extreme bacon lover and has passed his love of bacon on to my children, thus bacon, for days. If you've ever cooked a whole pork tenderloin and had it come out so dry that you feel like your jaw is going to fall off when you chew, then you're doing it all wrong. One word: bacon. Wrap that sucker in bacon, and it seals in all the juices, keeping this pork so moist and so juicy, plus—bacon crust! Marinate this pork for at least 3 hours, but if you can think ahead, try marinating overnight for ultimate flavor.

YIELD: 6 SERVINGS

2 ½ lbs (1 kg) **pork tenderloin**, cut into 6 inch (15 cm) pieces
1 lb (455 g) thick-cut bacon
¾ c (180 ml) **soy sauce**
2 tbsp (25 g) minced fresh **onion**
1 tsp garlic powder
1 tbsp (15 ml) **balsamic vinegar**
¼ tsp salt
¾ c (150 g) **brown sugar**

If you can, start marinating at least 3 hours prior to cooking!

Wrap the bacon in a crisscross pattern around the pork tenderloins, then use a fork and pierce the tenderloins all over, several times. Place in a 9"x 13" (23 x 33 cm) casserole dish and set aside.

Combine the remaining ingredients in a separate bowl and pour over the pork. Refrigerate, uncovered, for at least 3 hours or overnight. Use a spoon to baste the tops of the pork with the marinade on the bottom of the pan every hour or so.

Bake at 300°F (149°C) for 1 ½ to 2 hours, or until the center of the pork reaches 145°F (63°C). If the bacon begins to burn, cover the pork loosely with foil. Carefully cut the pork into pieces and serve with any extra juices on the bottom of the pan.

SWEET AND SOUR PORK STIR-FRY

To be honest, I used to dislike pork tenderloin. I won't say "hate," because "hate" is a strong word that I reserve for things like "taxes" and "folding laundry." Nope, I was never a huge fan of pork tenderloin because it always seemed to dry out on me. Then there was that one time that a glass baking dish exploded in my oven while I was baking a pork tenderloin. Was it a sign, or just cheap bakeware? Who knows?! I have, however, discovered a new love for pork tenderloin, and it all stems from this recipe. The pork in this sweet and sour stir-fry is, well, tender and moist thanks to the quick searing in the hot wok. Mixed with the sweet and sour sauce, it's the perfect quick dinner to win your skeptical pork-loving heart over! Serve it over a bed of white rice and garnish with green onions for a complete meal.

YIELD: 4 SERVINGS

1 lb (455 g) **pork tenderloin**, cut into ½ inch (1.3 cm) rounds, then cut into ½ inch (1.3 cm) strips

Salt and pepper

1 tbsp (8 g) + 1 tsp cornstarch, divided

2 tbsp (30 ml) olive oil, divided

1 **onion**, sliced into thin strips

¼ c (60 ml) **balsamic vinegar**

4 tbsp (50 g) **brown sugar**

1 tsp **soy sauce**

1 tbsp (15 ml) ketchup

4 tsp (20 ml) + 1 tbsp (15 ml) water

Optional additions: white rice and sliced green onions

Season the pork strips with salt and pepper then toss them in the 1 tablespoon (8 g) cornstarch.

Add 1 tablespoon (15 ml) of olive oil to a large skillet or wok and heat over medium-high heat, until the oil is hot. Brown half of the pork strips on all sides, for about 2 to 3 minutes, then remove from the wok and keep warm. Repeat with the remaining oil and pork strips, then remove from the wok and keep warm.

Throw in the onion strips and stir-fry until they begin to soften a little and become translucent.

Meanwhile, whisk together the balsamic vinegar, brown sugar, soy sauce, ketchup and 4 teaspoons (20 ml) of water in a small bowl. Once the onions are cooked, add the sauce ingredients to the wok and reduce the heat to medium. Thicken the sauce by mixing 1 teaspoon of cornstarch with 1 tablespoon (15 ml) of water in a small bowl and then add it to the wok. Once the mixture thickens slightly, add the pork strips back to the wok and stir to coat.

Variations: I love adding extra veggies to my stir-fry. You can try sliced red bell peppers, snow peas or matchstick carrots to bulk up this family-friendly dish.

STACKED BBQ PULLED PORK NACHOS

These next three recipes are my favorite quickie meals. They are no-brainer meals, which are perfect for busy weeknights and also tasty hot lunches!

Nachos are a special thing in our house. We have a tradition that every Sunday after church, we come home and prepare a large pan of piping hot nachos. Some people in our family would say that it's something they look forward to all week long. Ahem, children. I'm not joking, my kids run on nacho time. As soon as we buckle up and start heading home, they start asking for nachos. I don't blame them though, who could resist a hot pile of melted cheese, shredded BBQ pork, fajita peppers and onions all on top of some crisp homemade tortilla chips? These nachos are a fun twist to the classic Mexican flavors, but still pair very well with sour cream and chopped cilantro on top.

YIELD: 4 SERVINGS

8 large **tortillas**

1 tbsp (15 ml) olive oil

¼ tsp salt

1 ½ c (130 g) **frozen fajita peppers and onions**—found in the freezer section

1 ½ c (375 g) **refrigerated BBQ pulled pork**, found in the deli section

2 c (225 g) **Mexican 3 cheese blend**, such as Kraft

3 tbsp (45 ml) **BBQ sauce**, warmed

Optional toppings: sour cream, chopped cilantro

Preheat the oven to 425°F (219°C).

Cut the tortillas into small triangles and toss with the olive oil and salt. Spread the tortilla triangles in an even layer on a baking sheet. Bake for 5 to 7 minutes or until browned and crisp.

Meanwhile, heat a large, heavy-bottomed skillet—I prefer my cast iron skillet here—over medium-high heat, until the skillet begins to smoke slightly. Add the frozen peppers and onions to the skillet and cook, stirring every 20 to 30 seconds until the peppers and onions are heated through and begin to char slightly, about 4 to 5 minutes.

While the peppers are cooking, heat up the BBQ pulled pork in the microwave according to package instructions.

To assemble the nachos, lay chips in the bottom of an oven-safe dish or baking sheet and layer on some pulled pork, fajita peppers and onions and Mexican cheese. Repeat the layers, ending with cheese on top, then bake at 425°F (219°C) for 5 to 7 minutes, or until the cheese is nice and melted.

Drizzle with the warmed BBQ sauce and top with any additional toppings you want.

Shawn's Quick Tip: Use store-bought tortilla chips for a quick nacho fix.

BBQ PULLED PORK FLAUTAS

Flautas are a lot like taquitos, but instead of using a corn tortilla and being fried, these flautas are made with flour tortillas and baked until crisp. While I love me some taquitos, flautas are great for stuffing with all sorts of cheesy fillings, and since we're baking these, there is much less of a mess to deal with. Plus they're great for using up leftovers such as shredded pork, taco meat or rotisserie chicken. To achieve the crisp outer shell, be sure to spritz with a little cooking spray prior to baking!

YIELD: 4 SERVINGS

3 c (750 g) **refrigerated BBQ pulled pork**—found in the deli section

8 large **tortillas**

2 c (170 g) **frozen fajita peppers and onions**—found in the freezer section

2 c (225 g) **Mexican 3 cheese blend**, such as Kraft

4 tbsp (60 ml) **BBQ sauce**

Cooking spray

Preheat the oven to 425°F (219°C).

Heat the BBQ pulled pork in the microwave according to package instructions. Place 4 tablespoons (65 g) of pulled pork down the center of each tortilla, then top with ¼ cup (20 g) of fajita peppers and onions mix and ¼ cup (30 g) of Mexican 3 cheese blend.

Roll each tortilla up and place seam-side down on a baking sheet lightly coated with cooking spray. Spritz the tops of the flautas with cooking spray and bake for 12 minutes; turn the flautas over and bake for an additional 5 minutes, until evenly browned. Serve with a side of BBQ sauce for dipping.

Variation: Try this Italian twist: Use 3 cups (420 g) shredded rotisserie chicken in place of the pulled pork and toss it in 1 cup (240 ml) marinara sauce. Switch out the Mexican Cheese blend for a shredded mozzarella, and proceed with the recipe as above. Dip them in extra marinara sauce if desired.

BBQ PORK TORTILLA PIZZA

I love a thin crust pizza, and by using a tortilla for this pizza's base, you get just that—a light, crispy thin crust. I'm always making this easy pizza for lunch, and when I run out of the pulled pork I substitute it with leftover grilled chicken. You can't go wrong with this one!

YIELD: 2 SERVINGS

2 large **tortillas**

2 tbsp (30 ml) **BBQ sauce**

1 ½ c (375 g) **refrigerated BBQ pulled pork**—found in the deli section

1 c (85 g) **frozen fajita peppers and onions**—found in the freezer section

1 ½ c (170 g) **Mexican 3 cheese blend**, such as Kraft

Preheat the oven to 425°F (219°C).

Lay 2 large tortillas on a pizza pan and spread the BBQ sauce over each tortilla, leaving just a bit of tortilla showing around the outside edge in true pizza fashion.

Warm up the BBQ pulled pork in the microwave according to package instructions, and then divide between the two tortillas in a thin layer. Top each tortilla pizza with the fajita peppers and onions—these can still be frozen—and then sprinkle with the cheese.

Bake for 5 to 6 minutes or until the cheese is melted and bubbly and the tortillas are lightly browned and crisp. Let the pizzas cool slightly before slicing into four wedges.

Shawn's Tip: For a crispier crust, use a pizza pan that has tiny holes on the bottom of it to allow air to reach the bottom of the tortillas.

LEMON THYME PORK CHOPS ON A STICK WITH BRUSSELS SPROUT AND APPLE SLAW

I love pairing a hot piece of meat with a cool and refreshing salad, and that's exactly what I did here. First of all, pork on a stick—yes. Secondly, hiding brussels sprouts in a cool and creamy slaw—brilliant. If you're on the fence with brussels sprouts, this delicious dish will push you over to "fan status." If it doesn't, I'm not sure we can be friends anymore.

YIELD: 4 SERVINGS

4 (6 oz [170 g]) boneless **pork loin chops**, 1-inch (2.5 cm) thick

1 tsp **lemon peel**

¼ c (60 ml) **lemon juice**

¼ c (60 ml) olive oil

1 tbsp (15 g) finely minced **purple onion**

1 tbsp (3 g) fresh thyme (or ½ tbsp [2 g] dried)

1 tsp garlic powder

½ tsp black pepper

¼ tsp salt

8 skewers

FOR THE BRUSSELS SPROUT AND APPLE SLAW

½ lb (230 g) **brussels sprouts**, trimmed

1 large Gala or Fuji **apple**, cored and thinly sliced

½ **purple onion**, thinly sliced

½ c (110 g) mayonnaise

1 tbsp (15 ml) **lemon juice**

1 tbsp (15 g) sugar

¼ tsp salt

Pinch of black pepper

Cut the pork chops in half, lengthwise, to get 8 pieces of pork. Combine the remaining ingredients, up until the skewers, in a large zip-top bag and shake to mix. Add the pork chops to the bag and let marinade in the fridge for 3 to 4 hours, turning the bag over occasionally.

If using wooden skewers, make sure to soak them in water for at least 20 minutes before grilling. Skewer the marinated pork chops onto the skewers and grill over medium heat for 7 to 9 minutes, turning halfway through.

Meanwhile, prepare the brussels sprout and apple slaw by finely shredding the trimmed brussels sprouts and combining with the sliced apple and onion in a large bowl. In a separate bowl, whisk together the remaining ingredients until smooth, then pour over the slaw and stir to combine. Serve the hot pork chops with the cool slaw.

Shawn's Quick Tip: If you have a food processor with a top-loading chute, use that to quickly and efficiently shred the brussels sprouts and apple slices. Or you can use a mandoline, but those things scare me.

GRILLED PORK CHOPS WITH A SWEET PAN-ROASTED HASH

I have memories from my childhood where my parents would introduce a new food to my older siblings and me. We could either take a bite or take a nap. I was always an adventurous little eater when I was younger; so when my parents introduced us kids to brussels sprouts, I had no trouble eating them. My siblings, on the other hand, they took naps. I suppose I'm lucky to have 4 adventurous little eaters of my own because they have no qualms when it comes to trying new foods such as this Sweet Pan-Roasted Hash. I've sautéed the brussels sprouts WITH the apples and onions until they char slightly, and then I bring in a little lemon and just a touch of cinnamon and butter to give it the taste of a warm applesauce. It's the perfect pairing to a thick and juicy grilled pork chop!

YIELD: 4 SERVINGS

4 (6 oz to 8 oz [170 g to 230 g]) bone-in **pork chops**, 1-inch (2.5 cm) thick

2 cloves garlic, pressed, or finely minced

2 tbsp (10 g) dried basil

2 tbsp (30 ml) **lemon juice**

2 tbsp (30 ml) olive oil

1 tsp salt

½ tsp black pepper

FOR THE SWEET PAN-ROASTED HASH

2 tsp (10 ml) olive oil

10 **brussels sprouts**, trimmed and quartered

2 Gala or Fuji **apples**, cored and chopped into bite-size pieces

½ **purple onion**, chopped

Juice of ½ **lemon**

2 dashes of cinnamon

2 tbsp (30 g) butter

Salt and pepper

Place the pork chops in a shallow dish. Combine the garlic, basil, lemon juice, olive oil, salt and black pepper in a small bowl and then pour over the pork chops, turning to coat. Let the pork chops sit on the counter for 15 minutes before grilling over medium heat for 7 to 9 minutes.

While the pork chops marinate, prepare the Sweet Pan-Roasted Hash by heating the olive oil in a large, heavy-bottomed skillet—I love my castiron skillet for this—over medium heat. Toss in the brussels sprouts, apples and onion and let them cook for 5 to 6 minutes, stirring occasionally until they have charred slightly. Stir in the lemon juice and sprinkle with a couple dashes of cinnamon. Once the lemon juice has nearly evaporated, add the butter and stir until melted. Remove from the heat and season with salt and pepper to taste. Serve with the grilled pork chops on top!

LEMON PORK SCHNITZEL WITH OVEN ROASTED BRUSSELS SPROUTS

I learned all about Schnitzels when I was living in Canada. Unlike the "Weiner Schnitzel" I grew up with in California, a pork schnitzel is a thinly pounded pork chop that's been quickly coated with breadcrumbs then pan-fried until crisp. Every diner in the small town we lived in actually had at least 4 different types of schnitzel to choose from. I've infused this pork schnitzel with lemon and then topped it with matchstick apples, which my kids call apple fries, to give it a sweet little crunch with each bite.

YIELD: 4 SERVINGS

1 lb (455 g) **brussels sprouts**, trimmed and halved

1 **purple onion**, chopped

1 c (240 ml) vegetable or canola oil, divided

Salt and pepper

½ c (65 g) flour

1 tsp Italian seasoning

½ tsp salt

¼ tsp black pepper

2 large eggs

1 tbsp (15 ml) **lemon juice**

1 c (120 g) plain breadcrumbs

1 tsp **lemon zest**

4 (6 oz [170 g]) boneless **pork chops**, pounded to ¼-inch (6 mm) thickness

1 Gala or Fuji **apple**, cut into matchsticks

Preheat the oven to 425°F (219°C).

Toss the brussels sprouts and chopped onion with 2 tablespoons (30 ml) vegetable oil, then season with salt and pepper to taste. Spread the vegetables onto a large baking sheet into an even layer. Roast in the oven for 20 to 25 minutes, stirring halfway, until the brussels sprouts have charred and the onions have softened.

Meanwhile, combine the flour, Italian seasoning and salt and pepper in a shallow dish, and set aside. Whisk together the eggs and lemon juice in another shallow dish, set aside. In a third shallow dish, toss together the breadcrumbs and lemon zest.

Add the remaining oil to a large, heavy-bottomed skillet over medium heat. Dredge each pork chop in the flour, then dip into the egg mixture; let any excess drip off and then dip the pork chop into the breadcrumbs to coat. Add the pork chops to the hot oil and fry on each side until golden brown, about 3 to 4 minutes.

Top each pork schnitzel with ¼ of the apple matchsticks, and squeeze a little extra lemon juice on top to keep the apples from turning brown.

Variation: This recipe would also work really well with chicken! Make sure to pound the chicken breast to a thin, even layer then proceed with the recipe as follows.

POLKA DOT LASAGNA SKILLET

Fennel seeds are one of those spices in your pantry that constantly get overlooked. One of my favorite things to do is crush the seeds in my pestle and mortar—a rolling pin or heavy skillet will work too—which releases an immense amount of aromatic flavor. Add the crushed fennel to some ground beef to give it a nice sausage-like taste. You're going to love this simple one-skillet rendition of this classic Italian dish.

YIELD: 6 SERVINGS

1 lb (455 g) **ground beef**

1 tsp fennel, crushed

1 ½ tsp (5 g) garlic powder, divided

1 tsp onion powder

2 c (240 ml) **pasta sauce**

2 c (210 g) **bowtie pasta**, uncooked

2 ½ c (600 ml) water

Pinch of red pepper flakes

½ c (125 g) **ricotta cheese**

1 egg

½ c (50 g) **Parmesan cheese**

1 tsp dried basil

2 tbsp (15 g) flour

½ tsp salt

⅛ tsp black pepper

Brown the ground beef in a large skillet and drain any excess fat.

Return the skillet to the stove and add the crushed fennel, 1 teaspoon of the garlic and the onion powder, stirring until the beef mixture becomes slightly fragrant. Add the pasta sauce, uncooked pasta, water and red pepper flakes. Stir and bring the mixture to a boil, then reduce the heat to low and cover, simmering for about 18 to 20 minutes, or until the pasta is fully cooked.

Meanwhile, combine the ricotta, egg, Parmesan cheese, basil, flour, ½ teaspoon garlic powder, salt and pepper in a large bowl and mix until combined. Scoop large dollops of the cheese mixture on top of the cooked pasta in the skillet, taking care to space them out.

Cover the lid and cook an additional 5 minutes, or until the cheese mixture has set.

Variation: I always keep a jar of basil pesto in my fridge and love using it in the cheese mixture of my lasagnas. Simply replace the dried basil in this recipe with 1 tablespoon (15 ml) of prepared basil pesto for a burst of flavor!

SLOW COOKER RICOTTA STUFFED MEATBALLS

There is something magical that happens when you introduce a stuffed meatball to a child. Well, at least to my children. I've never seen my kids so eagerly consume their food as when I make these Ricotta Stuffed Meatballs. They love taking a big bite of their meatballs and finding that cheesy center, and now I get yelled at whenever I make an "unstuffed" meatball. Sheesh!

YIELD: 6 SERVINGS

1 ½ lb (680 g) **ground beef**
½ c (60 g) plain breadcrumbs
1 tsp Italian seasoning
½ tsp garlic powder
½ tsp onion powder
1 tsp dried parsley
2 tbsp (30 ml) milk
1 ½ tsp (8 g) salt, divided
½ tsp black pepper, divided
1 cup (250 g) **ricotta cheese**
½ c (50 g) **Parmesan cheese**
1 (29 oz [860 ml]) can **pasta sauce**
1 lb (455 g) **bowtie pasta**, cooked according to package instructions

Combine the ground beef, breadcrumbs, Italian seasoning, garlic powder, onion powder, dried parsley, milk, ¼ teaspoon salt and ⅛ teaspoon black pepper to a large bowl. Use your hands to fully mix the seasonings with the meat. Form the meat into 1 ½ to 2 inch (4 to 5 cm) meatballs and set aside.

In a separate bowl, combine the ricotta, Parmesan cheese, remaining salt and black pepper and stir together. Pour the cheese mixture into a zip-top bag.

Grab the meatballs and use your finger to gently push a hole in the middle of each one, making sure to not push all the way through. Snip off the end of the zip-top bag and squeeze a little bit of the cheese mixture into each meatball, leaving enough room to pinch the meatballs closed, enclosing the cheese mixture. Save any leftover cheese mixture in the fridge until ready to serve.

Pour half of the pasta sauce into the bottom of your slow cooker and then gently place the meatballs in. Cover with the remaining spaghetti sauce and then cook, covered, on low for 6 hours.

Serve the meatballs and sauce over the prepared pasta, and use the leftover cheese mixture to place a teaspoon on top of each meatball, which makes for a pretty presentation.

Variation: Give these meatballs an ultra cheesy gooey center by adding ½ cup (60 g) of shredded mozzarella cheese to the ricotta mixture before filling the meatballs!

PASTA BALLS WITH MEAT SAUCE

I've taken the classic "Spaghetti and Meatballs," and flipped them upside down with this fun and quirky recipe. Sometimes my husband thinks I'm a little wacky when it comes to the recipes I dream up, but he really enjoys these crispy-edged pasta balls as much as I do. Serve them hot over a bowl of this hearty meat sauce, and you'll be hooked too.

YIELD: 4 SERVINGS

2 c (210 g) **bowtie pasta**, crushed
1 lb (455 g) **ground beef**
1 (29 oz [860 ml]) can **pasta sauce**
1 ½ tsp salt, divided
2 tsp (7 g) garlic powder, divided
1 tsp onion powder
¼ tsp black pepper
2 qt (2 L) canola oil
1 c (250 g) **ricotta cheese**
½ c (50 g) **Parmesan cheese**
1 egg, lightly beaten
1 c (120 g) panko breadcrumbs
1 tbsp (2 g) Italian seasoning

Start by boiling the crushed pasta in a large pot of lightly salted water. Once it's tender to bite, drain and rinse with cold water, and set it aside.

Get the meat sauce going by browning the ground beef in a large skillet, over medium heat, using a spoon to crumble the beef into little pieces. Drain any excess fat from the pan, return the pan to the stove and then stir in the pasta sauce, 1 teaspoon salt, 1 teaspoon garlic powder, onion powder and black pepper. Bring the sauce to a low boil, then reduce the heat and let simmer, stirring occasionally for 10 to 15 minutes, or until your spaghetti balls are ready.

Add the oil to a large heavy-bottomed pot or a deep fryer. Heat the oil to 375°F (191°C).

In a medium-size bowl, combine the cooked pasta, ricotta cheese, Parmesan cheese, egg, panko breadcrumbs, Italian seasoning, 1 teaspoon garlic powder and ½ teaspoon salt. Firmly form the mixture into small balls (about 1 inch [2.5 cm] in diameter), and then gently place into the preheated oil, letting them cook for about 2 to 3 minutes, or until they have turned a light golden brown. Remove from the oil with a slotted spoon and let drain on a paper towel–lined plate.

To serve, place a cup of the meat sauce on a plate and top with the hot pasta balls.

Shawn's Tip: I use a sharp-edged cookie scoop to form my pasta balls, and then place the ball in the palm of my hand and give it a nice squeeze to make sure it holds together in the fryer.

CARNE ASADA
WITH GRILLED MINI SWEET PEPPERS

I grew up in Arizona, just north of the Mexican border. With at least 5 Mexican restaurants within walking distance, I quickly adopted the bright and bold flavors of our southern neighbors. We had this tiny Mexican drive-thru just around the corner from my house, and one of my favorite things to order was the Carne Asada. The key to a delicious Carne Asada is to let it marinate, but not for too long or the steak will become tough. This tender meat begs to be served inside of a warm tortilla with all the taco trimmings!

YIELD: 6 SERVINGS

2 lb (910 g) **flank steak**

½ c (120 ml) olive oil

Juice of 2 **limes**

2 **purple onions**, one diced and one sliced into rings

1 **jalapeño**, seeds removed and diced

1 tsp cumin

½ c (8 g) chopped cilantro

½ tsp salt

½ tsp black pepper

12 **mini sweet peppers**, in assorted colors

Place the flank steak in a large shallow dish and set aside.

In a medium bowl, mix together the olive oil, lime juice, 1 diced purple onion, diced jalapeño, cumin, cilantro, salt and pepper. Pour the marinade over the flank steak, turning to coat. Cover with plastic wrap and let marinate in the fridge for 1 to 4 hours, turning once halfway. Let the steak come to room temperature, usually about 20 minutes, and then heat the grill over high heat. You want the grill super-hot so you get a great sear on the steak, which locks in the juices.

Remove the steak from the marinade, brushing off any onions or cilantro that decide to stick to it (those will just burn).

Once the grill is hot, place your steak, peppers—yes, the whole pepper—and sliced onions onto the grill. Let the steak cook for 3 to 5 minutes per side for a medium doneness, or longer until desired temperature is reached. Turn the peppers and onions occasionally until the skins become slightly charred and blackened.

Remove the steak from the grill and let rest for 5 minutes, then slice against the grain into ¼-inch-thick pieces. Serve hot with the grilled peppers and onions.

Shawn's Grilling Tip: Always let your meats come to room temperature before grilling! This will allow the meat to be cooked evenly. Also, always allow your meat to rest for at least 5 minutes before slicing, so the juices inside of the meat will have a chance to redistribute, resulting in a tender, juicy piece of meat.

CILANTRO LIME CHIMICHURRI STEAK ROLLS

Believe it or not, I was living in Kansas when I was first introduced to a chimichurri sauce. Chimichurri is a lot like a pesto, but instead of fresh basil, parsley is used and then brightened up with vinegar. Well, I subbed out the parsley for cilantro and gave this beautiful green sauce a nice zip with some freshly squeezed lime juice. It's the perfect topping to these adorable pepper-filled steak bundles!

YIELD: 4 SERVINGS

1 lb (455 g) **flank steak**
3 tbsp (45 ml) olive oil, divided
½ of a **lime**, juiced
Salt and pepper
6 **mini sweet peppers**, in assorted colors, thinly sliced
2 **jalapeños**, seeded and thinly sliced
1 **purple onion**, halved and thinly sliced
½ tsp garlic powder

FOR THE SAUCE
½ c (120 ml) olive oil
¼ c (60 ml) **lime juice**
½ c (8 g) cilantro
½ tsp salt
½ **jalapeño**, seeded
1 tsp garlic powder

In order to make these rolls, we'll need to pound the steak into a thin layer. Place the steak between two sheets of parchment paper and use a meat mallet or a heavy rolling pin and pound the steak until it's about ¼ inch (6 mm) thick all over. Cut the steaks into 3-inch-wide by at least 6-inch-long (8 cm x 16 cm) strips and place in a shallow pan.

In a small bowl, combine 1 tablespoon (15 ml) olive oil, the lime juice, salt and pepper to taste, and pour the mixture over the steak strips. Let the steak marinate for 30 minutes.

Meanwhile, heat a large heavy skillet over medium heat. Add the thinly sliced peppers and onion to the hot skillet and stir-fry for 5 to 6 minutes or until the peppers have charred slightly and become tender-crisp. Season the peppers with the garlic powder and salt and pepper to taste, and then remove from the skillet to a clean bowl.

Remove the steaks from the marinade and lay flat. Place 2 tablespoons (15 g) of peppers in the center of each steak strip and roll up, securing with a toothpick.

Heat the remaining 2 tablespoons (30 ml) of oil in the large heavy skillet that the peppers were cooked in, over medium-high heat. Carefully place each steak roll in the hot pan, cooking for 3 minutes, turning halfway through to brown all sides.

To prepare the sauce, combine all the sauce ingredients in a blender or food processor and blend until smooth. Serve the sauce drizzled on top of the steak rolls.

Variation: For an Italian twist, switch out the mini sweet peppers and jalapeños with equal amounts sliced zucchini and matchstick carrots. Make a quick pesto sauce (page 53) to drizzle over the steaks.

SPICY BEEF STIR-FRY

Stir-fries are one of my signature go-to dishes at home. I love gazing into my fridge and pulling out all the leftover produce—you know what I'm talking about, the half-used bell pepper and quarter of an onion hanging out in the back of your veggie drawer—and combining them all together with a beautiful sauce for a quick and easy dinner. This spicy beef stir-fry can be tamed down in heat by simply removing the seeds to the jalapeños, but I love the contrast between the sweet peppers and the spicy jalapeño. Between that and the tangy lime sauce, it's a flavor explosion in your mouth!

YIELD: 4 SERVINGS

½ c (65 g) all purpose flour

½ tsp salt

½ tsp pepper

1 lb (455 g) **flank steak**, thinly sliced against the grain

¼ c (60 ml) olive oil

6 **mini sweet peppers**, thinly sliced into rings

1 **jalapeño**, thinly sliced into rings, remove the seeds to tame the spice

½ **purple onion**, thinly sliced

½ tsp cumin

2 **limes**, zested and juiced

½ c (120 ml) water

½ c (8 g) cilantro, roughly chopped

Optional: white rice for serving

Place the flour in a shallow dish and add the salt and pepper. Toss the steak strips in the flour, shaking off any excess.

Heat the olive oil in a large skillet over medium heat and add the steak strips in batches to the hot pan, cooking for 1 to 2 minutes, turning halfway. You don't want to overcrowd the pan, so it may take a couple batches to get through all the strips. Add more oil to the pan if necessary. Once the steak is cooked, remove from the pan and keep warm.

Toss the peppers and onion slices into the same skillet, along with the cumin, and sauté for 3 to 4 minutes until tender. Add the lime juice, zest and water to the pan. Scrape any browned bits from the bottom of the pan—it adds tremendous flavor to the sauce, trust me. Once the sauce has thickened slightly, about 2 to 3 minutes, return the cooked beef strips the pan and toss in the sauce. Before serving, toss in the chopped cilantro and serve over white rice if desired.

Shawn's Quick Tip: Slicing thin strips of steak can be tricky with a floppy piece of meat. Firm up your steak in the freezer for 10 to 15 minutes for easy slicing!

GRILLED TENDERLOIN STEAKS OVER CREAMY SPINACH SAUCE

This is one of those fancy dishes that you can make for your loved ones to truly impress them with your cooking skills. They don't need to know that this recipe is actually extremely easy to prepare. We can keep that our little secret. My husband gets all glossy-eyed whenever he sees this beautiful dish on our dinner table, and as an added bonus, my kids can't get enough of that creamy spinach sauce!

YIELD: 4 SERVINGS

2 tbsp (30 ml) olive oil, divided
8 oz (230 g) baby **spinach** leaves
2 tbsp (30 g) butter
2 tbsp (15 g) flour
1 ½ c (355 ml) milk
½ c (75 g) **feta cheese**, crumbled
1 tbsp (1 g) freshly chopped **dill**
1 tsp garlic powder
4 (6 oz [170 g]) **tenderloin steaks**
Salt and pepper
1 **tomato**, diced

Heat 1 tablespoon (15 ml) olive oil in a large pan over medium heat, then gradually add the baby spinach leaves, stirring until the leaves have wilted and cooked down. Drain the spinach in a fine mesh strainer and press with paper towels to remove any excess moisture. Chop the spinach and set aside.

Return the pan to the heat and melt the butter over medium heat. Whisk in the flour until a thick paste forms, then slowly add the milk, while constantly whisking until the mixture is smooth. Add the feta, spinach, dill and garlic powder to the pan and bring to a light bubble. Reduce the heat to low and let simmer until the mixture thickens.

Meanwhile, brush the grill racks with the remaining 1 tablespoon (15 ml) olive oil and heat the grill to medium-high. Season the steaks with salt and pepper, then grill the steaks for 3 to 4 minutes per side, or until desired doneness is reached. Let the steaks rest for 5 minutes before slicing into thin strips.

Place a cup of the spinach sauce on a plate, top with the steak strips, diced tomato and extra feta cheese if desired.

Shawn's Quick Tip: Use a package of frozen spinach in place of the fresh spinach to save time. Just let it thaw, and then squeeze it dry to remove any excess moisture.

PAN SEARED GREEK STEAKS WITH STUFFED TOMATOES

Spanakopita has been one of my favorite Greek side dishes ever since I was introduced to the spinach-filled pie while living in Houston, Texas. I know, *who eats Greek food in Texas?!* This gal. While I love the crispy and flaky phyllo crust of the traditional spanakopita, I don't love the arduous task of working with the finicky dough. Instead, I opted to stuff the spinach and feta cheese filling into a plump tomato, which gives this delicious side dish a juicy bite, and pairs wonderfully with these Greek–inspired steaks!

YIELD: 4 SERVINGS

2 tbsp (30 ml) olive oil, divided

2 tsp (10 ml) red wine vinegar

½ tsp garlic powder

½ tsp finely chopped **dill**

4 (6 oz [170 g]) **tenderloin steaks**

4 large hothouse **tomatoes**

13 oz (370 g) **spinach**, cooked down, and squeezed dry

¼ tsp salt

⅛ tsp pepper

1 tsp dried oregano

1 tsp dried basil

1 tsp fresh **dill**

1 egg, lightly beaten

1 tbsp (15 ml) lemon juice

1 c (150 g) crumbled **feta cheese**

Preheat the oven to 350°F (177°C).

Combine 1 tablespoon (15 ml) olive oil, red wine vinegar, garlic powder, and chopped dill in a large zip-top bag and shake to mix. Place the steaks in the bag, seal and let marinate on the countertop for 20 minutes.

Meanwhile, cut the tops off the tomatoes and use a melon baller or a sharp spoon to scoop out the seeds of the tomatoes, creating a "tomato cup." Combine the remaining ingredients in a large bowl and mix together. Scoop the filling into each tomato and place on a foil-lined baking sheet. Bake the tomatoes for 15 to 17 minutes or until the tops are lightly browned.

Meanwhile, heat a large, heavy-bottomed, oven-safe skillet on the stovetop over medium-high heat. Add 1 tablespoon (15 ml) of oil to the pan and sear the steaks for 2 to 3 minutes per side, then finish cooking in the oven for 5 minutes, or until the steak reaches your desired doneness. Let the steak rest for 5 minutes before slicing, and serve with the stuffed tomatoes.

Shawn's Tip: If the tomatoes don't want to stand up on their own, use a sharp knife and carefully make a flat slice on the bottom of the tomatoes, but not all the way through, so it's not exposing the filling inside.

Must make sauce: It might just be me, but I always serve my Greek food with a side of Tzatziki sauce. Here's my quick recipe: ½ cup (100 g) plain Greek yogurt, 2 tablespoons (20 g) chopped cucumber, 1 teaspoon fresh dill, 1 tablespoon (15 ml) lemon juice, salt and pepper to taste. Combine all the sauce ingredients in a bowl and whisk together.

GRILLED STEAK SALAD WITH CREAMY FETA VINAIGRETTE

One of the perks of being a food blogger is being whisked away by brands and being showered with all sorts of delicious foods. Once I was working with the Arizona Beef Council and was taken on a tour of some local cattle ranches in the desert. As the sun was about to set with a gorgeous pink and purple sky, a private chef prepared a grilled steak salad for us. The combination of warm grilled steak on top of cool greens all married together with a tangy vinaigrette dressing is my idea of awesome. And I'm not just saying that because I was surrounded by cowboys and cactuses.

YIELD: 4 SERVINGS

½ c (75 g) crumbled **feta cheese**

1 ½ tsp freshly chopped **dill**

2 tbsp (30 ml) red wine vinegar

3 tbsp (45 ml) olive oil, divided

4 tbsp (60 ml) cold water

4 (6 oz [170 g]) **tenderloin steaks**

Salt and pepper

1 (10 oz [285 g]) package baby **spinach** leaves

2 **tomatoes**, sliced into wedges

Combine the crumbled feta, dill, red wine vinegar and 2 tablespoons (30 ml) of olive oil in a small bowl. Use a fork to mash the ingredients together. Pour the mixture into a salad dressing shaker and add the cold water, shaking to combine. Set aside.

Brush the steaks with the remaining tablespoon (15 ml) of olive oil and season with salt and pepper. Grill the steaks over medium-high heat for 3 to 4 minutes per side. Let the steak rest for 5 minutes before slicing into thin strips.

Place 2 cups (60 g) of baby spinach leaves on each plate, top with steak strips and tomato wedges and drizzle with the creamy feta dressing.

Variation: This steak salad would work great with a flank steak or skirt steak as well. Just be sure to cut the steak strips against the grain to achieve a tender bite similar to the tenderloin steak.

ROASTED STEAK AND ROOT VEGETABLES

I'll never forget the first time I attempted to roast vegetables in the oven. It was Thanksgiving, and I was visiting my sister-in-law's house. I was given the task of making cauliflower and broccoli, and I wanted to impress with this new trendy thing called "roasted cauliflower." Long story short, the whole house smelled of burnt oil, and the broccoli and cauliflower tasted bitter and awful. A few key things to keep in mind when roasting is to get your oven hot before adding the vegetables, and to make sure everything is coated in a thin layer of oil. Now that I'm a roasting pro, I love to roast carrots to bring out their sweet taste. This whole *one-skillet* dinner is a sure way to impress!

YIELD: 4 SERVINGS

4 (1 ½-inch [3.7 cm] thick) **sirloin steaks**

Salt and pepper

½ tsp dried oregano

3 tbsp (42 g) butter, divided

2 tbsp (30 ml) olive oil, divided

2 medium **carrots** cut into 2-inch (5 cm) strips

2 medium **parsnips**, cut into 1-inch (2.5 cm) pieces

1 medium **onion**, sliced into rings

1 lb (455 g) **asparagus**, trimmed

½ tsp salt

2 tsp (10 ml) balsamic vinegar

Preheat the oven to 425°F (219°C). Use a 12" (30 cm) cast iron skillet (or something similar that can be placed into a hot oven).

Season the steaks with salt and pepper and sprinkle with the dried oregano.

Heat the skillet over medium-high heat and add 1 tablespoon (15 g) of butter and 1 tablespoon (15 ml) of olive oil. Add the steaks to the hot skillet and do not touch the steaks for 2 minutes, then flip the steaks and let brown on the other side. Transfer the steaks to a large plate and set aside.

Add the remaining olive oil to the pan, add the veggies and sprinkle with ½ teaspoon salt, more if desired. Then toss to coat the veggies in the olive oil and spread into an even layer.

Place the skillet into the hot oven and roast for 15 minutes or until tender. Set the steaks on top of the veggies and return the pan to the oven for an additional 7 to 10 minutes or until the steaks are cooked to your liking.

Let the steaks rest for 5 minutes before slicing, and toss the veggies with the remaining 2 tablespoons (30 g) of butter and balsamic vinegar.

Shawn's Roasting Tip: If you don't have a large-enough cast iron skillet to fit 4 steaks, sear the steaks one at a time on the stovetop, and then use a large, shallow-rimmed baking sheet to roast the veggies in the oven. Place the steaks on top of the baking sheet after the veggies have cooked for the first 15 minutes, and proceed with the recipe.

RUSTIC BEEF STEW

When I had my first "real winter" in Canada, I was absolutely addicted to warm, hearty soups and stews.
I got a lot of mileage out of my large, red, ceramic Dutch oven on those cold, dark winter nights.
I love this hearty stew, especially toward the end of fall when the carrots in my garden
are at their peak. Serve this warming stew with a side of crusty bread!

YIELD: 6 SERVINGS

1 tbsp (15 ml) olive oil

1 lb (455 g) **sirloin steak**, cut into 1-inch (2.5 cm) pieces

1 ½ tsp (8 g) salt, divided

⅛ tsp black pepper

3 c (710 ml) beef broth

2 medium **carrots**, cut into 1-inch (2.5 cm) pieces

2 medium **parsnips**, cut into 1-inch (2.5 cm) pieces

½ lb (230 g) **asparagus**, trimmed and cut into 1-inch (2.5 cm) pieces

1 small **onion**, chopped

1 bay leaf

½ c (120 ml) cold water

2 tbsp (15 g) flour

Heat a large Dutch oven over medium heat and add the olive oil. Season the steak with ½ teaspoon salt and the black pepper, then add to the hot oil to brown the steak on all sides, locking in the juices, about 3 to 4 minutes.

Pour in the beef broth and scrape any browned bits off the bottom of the pot. Bring the mixture to a small boil, then reduce the heat to low, cover and let simmer for 2 to 2 ½ hours.

Add the carrots, parsnips, asparagus, onion, 1 teaspoon salt and bay leaf to the pot, then cover and continue to simmer for 30 minutes or until the vegetables are tender.

Finally, remove the bay leaf and then whisk together the water and flour in a small bowl. Add the flour mixture to the stew and bring to a boil, stirring, until the mixture thickens slightly, about 2 minutes.

Variation: If you prefer a more traditional beef stew, you can sub 1 ½ cups (270 g) diced potatoes for parsnips and 1 cup (100 g) celery for asparagus.

CINNAMON GRILLED SIRLOIN & ASPARAGUS WITH A CARROT AND PARSNIP MASH

Ever since I can remember, grilling has been one of my favorite ways to prepare a steak. My parents bought my husband and I our first grill when we got married, and over the years, we have somehow collected 4 more different types of grills. Obviously, we're ready to throw one massive backyard grill fest if the need arises. When it comes to steak, salt and pepper is always a safe bet, but what about adding a little spice? How about a little bit of sweet cinnamon with a hint of paprika to give it a sweet and smoky kick? *I thinks me likes it a lot.* It's the perfect pairing to the creamy carrot and parsnip mash!

YIELD: 4 SERVINGS

1 tsp cumin
1 tbsp (15 g) brown sugar
1 tsp cinnamon
1 tsp oregano
1 tsp paprika
½ tsp salt
4 (1-inch [2.5 cm] thick) **sirloin steaks**
1 lb (455 g) **asparagus**, trimmed
2 tbsp (30 ml) olive oil
Salt and pepper
½ lb (230 g) **carrots,** coarsely chopped
1 lb (455 g) **parsnips,** coarsely chopped
5 tbsp (75 g) butter
Pinch of nutmeg

Combine the cumin, brown sugar, cinnamon, oregano, paprika and salt in a small bowl. Pat the steaks dry and coat the steaks with the dry spice rub. Cover the steaks and let marinate in the fridge for 1 hour.

Meanwhile, add the carrots to a large pot of salted water and bring to a boil. Boil for 5 minutes and then add the parsnips, and continue boiling for 15 more minutes, partially covered. Drain the carrots and parsnips in a strainer then place in a food processor with the butter, salt and pepper to taste, and a pinch of nutmeg. Process until smooth, taste and add more seasonings if necessary.

Heat the grill to high, and brush the grates with olive oil.

Toss the asparagus with the olive oil and season with salt and pepper. Grill the steaks over the hot grill, 2 to 4 minutes per side. Add the asparagus next to the steaks and turn occasionally to prevent burning.

Serve hot with the carrot and parsnip mash.

Variation: The aromatic spice rub would go great on any type of steak, so feel free to use your favorite cut of beef with this recipe!

CHEESY TACO PIZZA

"Pizza?! Now that's what I call a taco!" This cheesy pizza has been a favorite of my husband's ever since I started making it years ago. A crispy pizza crust topped with cheesy sauce, taco meat and all the fillings—better make two, since one never seems to be enough!

YIELD: 6 SERVINGS

1 (14 oz [390 g]) tube **pizza dough**, such as Pillsbury

1 lb (455 g) **ground beef**

½ white onion, diced, optional

1 (1 ¼-oz [35 g]) packet **taco seasoning**

¼ cup (60 ml) water

1 ½ c (360 g) jarred **queso cheese dip**, divided

1 (4 oz [130 ml]) can diced **green chiles**

Optional toppings: shredded lettuce, diced tomato, sliced black olives, sour cream, salsa

Preheat the oven to 400°F (205°C).

Open the pizza dough and press it out on a baking sheet to an even thickness, then par-bake—which is just fancy talk for "bake it halfway"—for 6 minutes.

While it's baking, combine the ground beef and diced onion in a large skillet over medium heat. Cook, stirring occasionally to brown the meat. Drain off any excess fat, then add the taco seasoning and water and stir to combine. Let simmer until the sauce has thickened slightly.

Once your pizza dough is half cooked, spread 1 cup (240 ml) of the cheese dip sauce over the top, then sprinkle the ground beef evenly all over the top, followed by the diced green chiles. Take the additional ½ cup (120 ml) cheese dip and drizzle it all over the top of the pizza.

Finish baking the pizza for 8 to 12 more minutes. Then feel free to top it off with all the optional toppings your heart desires!

Shawn's Tip: If your cheese sauce is too thick to drizzle over your pizza, just pop it in the microwave for 20 seconds, stir and then drizzle away!

TACO PIZZA POCKET

Okay, so these tacos don't have legs, but you do! And since the cheesy beefy mixture is tucked away nicely inside a pizza pocket, you're free to roam about eating tacos as you please. Whenever I make these, I double the recipe and stash a few in the freezer for my kids to take in their lunch box, which is a total win-win for me!

YIELD: 4 SERVINGS

2 (14 oz [390 g] each) tubes **pizza dough,** such as Pillsbury

½ lb (230 g) **ground beef**

1 tbsp (9 g) **taco seasoning**

2 tbsp (30 ml) water

2 tbsp (20 g) diced **green chiles**

8 tbsp (120 g) jarred **queso cheese dip**

1 tbsp (15 ml) milk

Optional garnish: sour cream and green onions

Preheat the oven to 425°F (219°C). Let the pizza dough sit on the counter for about 10 minutes to come up to room temperature.

Break up and brown the ground beef in a large skillet over medium-high heat, then drain any excess fat. Add the taco seasoning, water and the diced green chiles. Stir mixture until it thickens and is heated through.

Meanwhile, unroll the pizza dough and press into a thin, even layer. Use a 4" (10 cm) cookie cutter or a sharp-edged large bowl to cut 12 circles out of the dough—you should be able to get at least 6 out of each tube of pizza dough.

Spoon a tablespoon (15 g) of cheese dip slightly off center, onto each pizza circle and then top with a generous 2 tablespoons (30 g) of taco meat. Carefully fold the dough over the beef mixture and seal the edges by crimping with a fork. Place the pizza pockets on a parchment-lined baking sheet. Brush the tops with a little milk, then bake for 15 to 17 minutes or until they have achieved that golden brown status.

Variation: Turn these Taco Pizza Pockets into Saucy Pizza Pockets by using pizza sauce instead of the taco seasoning and green chiles. Top them with shredded mozzarella instead of cheese dip!

Money Saving Tip: Store any leftover pizza dough scraps in an airtight container in the fridge and use for the breadsticks that go along with the Mexican Wedding Soup (page 111).

MEXICAN WEDDING SOUP WITH GARLIC BREADSTICK TWISTS

I love doing twists on classic recipes. This soup is the Mexican version of a classic Italian Wedding soup—full of taco-seasoned meatballs, with ribbons of egg in a slightly cheesy, slightly spicy broth. It's the perfect way to warm up on a cool night!

YIELD: 8 SERVINGS

FOR THE SOUP

1 lb (455 g) **ground beef**

1 (1 ¼ oz [35 g]) packet **taco seasoning**

¼ c (30 g) plain breadcrumbs

¼ tsp salt

⅛ tsp black pepper

3 eggs, divided

2 tbsp (2 g) dried or fresh cilantro

10 c (2 ½ L) chicken broth

4 tbsp (60 g) jarred **queso cheese dip**

2 tbsp (20 g) canned, diced **green chiles**

FOR THE BREADSTICKS

1 (14 oz [390 g]) tube **pizza dough,** such as Pillsbury

2 tbsp (30 g) butter

1 tsp garlic powder

Preheat the oven to 425°F (219°C).

Combine the ground beef, taco seasoning, breadcrumbs, salt, pepper, 1 egg and cilantro in a large bowl, using your hands to combine the mixture. Form into balls about the size of a ping-pong ball, and set on a wax paper–lined baking sheet.

Meanwhile, bring the chicken broth to a low boil and gently add the meatballs. Let them cook for at least 8 minutes. In a small bowl, whisk together the remaining 2 eggs with the cheese dip until smooth. Slowly stir the soup in a clockwise motion while steadily drizzling in the egg mixture. The egg will cook into thin ribbons as it hits the hot soup. Add the green chiles and let simmer for 5 minutes.

For the breadsticks, unwrap the pizza dough and cut it in half width-wise, forming two squares. Cut each square into thin, 1-inch-wide (2.5 cm) strips.

Melt the butter and stir in the garlic powder. Use half the butter to brush on the long strips of pizza dough. Fold the dough in half, covering the buttered part, and twist. Place on a baking sheet and bake for 10 to 12 minutes or until golden brown, then immediately brush with the remaining butter mixture. Serve hot with the soup!

Variation: If you want to bulk up the soup, feel free to add 1 cup (140 g) of frozen or canned corn to the chicken broth before adding the meatballs. Then bring the mixture to a boil and proceed with the recipe.

CHAPTER THREE:

PLENTY OF FISH IN THE SEA

15 DELIGHTFULLY FRESH AND EASY SEAFOOD RECIPES

This chapter was one of my favorites to create. I have always been a fan of seafood, even when I was a small child. It's a love that has thankfully been passed down to my children too. Every New Year's Eve, my husband and I go all out and buy several pounds of crab legs and lobster tails. I'll even whip up some shrimp cocktail and Bacon Wrapped Scallops (page 130), too. It's a tradition that the whole family loves and really gets into.

You don't have to save seafood for special occasions though. Frozen shrimp and scallops can quickly be defrosted for a speedy weeknight dinner, such as my Home-Style Shrimp Bowls (page 142). They're filled with creamy mashed potatoes, corn and spicy shrimp, all ready in less than 30 minutes! With my Teriyaki Salmon Pouches (page 125) everyone will feel special opening up their own parcel filled with tender salmon and mixed Asian veggies. *Mmmm!*

Hopefully you'll find a few recipes in here that will become new family favorites in your home!

TOMATO ZUCCHINI RISOTTO WITH OVEN ROASTED SHRIMP

You'll feel like you've stepped into a 5-star restaurant when you taste this decadent dish. But what's even more impressive is how quickly it all comes together! Because the shrimp are roasted in the oven, they all cook evenly and are ready to go at the same time. And because we're cheating and using microwave risotto, we can plump it up with some shredded zucchini and loads of Parmesan cheese. The crispy pancetta sprinkled on top is a must, and truly completes this meal.

YIELD: 4 SERVINGS

2 (250 g each) packages Uncle Ben's *Bistro Express* **Tomato & Herb Risotto**

2 tsp (10 ml) olive oil

1 tsp smoked paprika

½ tsp salt

¼ tsp black pepper

1 lb (455 g) medium **shrimp**, peeled and deveined

4 slices **pancetta** style bacon, cut into small pieces

1 large **zucchini**, shredded

½ c (40 g) **Parmesan cheese**, shredded

Preheat the oven to 400°F (216°C). Line a large, rimmed baking sheet with parchment paper and set aside. Cook the risotto according to package instructions, and set aside.

In a large bowl, combine the olive oil, smoked paprika, salt and pepper and stir until combined. Add the shrimp to the bowl and stir to coat. Place the shrimp in an even layer on the parchment paper and bake in the oven for 5 minutes, or until the shrimp are cooked through.

Meanwhile, cook the pancetta in a large skillet until crisp, then use a slotted spoon to remove the pancetta from the skillet to a paper towel–lined plate. Toss the zucchini into the hot skillet and cook, stirring frequently for 2 minutes until the zucchini softens. Pour the prepared risotto into the skillet and stir to combine. Remove the skillet from the heat and stir in the Parmesan cheese.

Divide the risotto between 4 plates, top with the cooked shrimp and crispy pancetta and enjoy immediately.

Shawn's Tip: Risotto is one of those meals that needs to be enjoyed right away, because the rice has a tendency to become gummy when it cools. So be sure to have all your ingredients prepped and ready to go before starting to ensure optimal texture and enjoyment.

SHRIMP STUFFED ZUCCHINI BOATS

I have to give mad props to my 10-year-old daughter for helping me snap this picture of me holding these zucchini boats. Girl's got some talent! I took my love of stuffed peppers and zucchini and combined the two to make these shrimp-stuffed zucchini boats. With the help of the microwavable tomato and herb risotto, this complete meal gets pulled together quickly and effortlessly. Just be sure to pick some zucchini that are fairly straight!

YIELD: 4 SERVINGS

3 large **zucchini**, halved lengthwise, insides removed—reserve 1 c (200 g) of the insides

1 (250 g) package Uncle Ben's *Bistro Express* **Tomato & Herb Risotto**

¾ c (60 g) shredded **Parmesan cheese**, divided

½ lb (230 g) raw medium **shrimp**, peeled, deveined and tails removed, cut into thirds

4 slices **pancetta** style bacon, cut into small pieces

½ tsp garlic powder

½ tsp dried parsley

Optional garnish: fresh chopped parsley

Broil the zucchini flesh-side-down on a large baking sheet for 5 minutes, remove from the oven, then reduce the heat to 425°F (219°C).

Turn the zucchini-flesh-side up in a baking dish, and then prepare the filling.

Prepare the risotto according to package instructions. Combine the cooked risotto with ½ cup (40 g) of shredded Parmesan and the remaining ingredients in a large bowl. Chop up the reserved zucchini insides and add to the filling mixture. Divide the filling into each of the zucchini boats and then sprinkle with the remaining Parmesan cheese. Bake for 20 minutes and garnish with freshly chopped parsley if desired.

Variation: Try using a different flavor of ready rice in lieu of the Tomato & Herb Risotto, such as Creamy Four Cheese Rice or Garden Vegetable Rice.

GRILLED PANCETTA-WRAPPED SHRIMP WITH A ZUCCHINI RIBBON SALAD

Can we all just agree that zucchini is one extremely versatile vegetable? There is no end to what that amazing green vegetable can do, besides of course, growing in my garden. I'm always extremely jealous of those who are overloaded with fresh zucchini in the late summer months, while my zucchini plants refuse to partake in such festivities. Such is life. With just a quick flick of the wrist and a trusty vegetable peeler, you can enjoy thin ribbons of zucchini, which when paired with a simple olive oil and vinegar dressing, become a light and refreshing side salad. It's the perfect accompaniment to these grilled pancetta-wrapped shrimp!

YIELD: 4 SERVINGS

24 medium **shrimp**, peeled and deveined

3 tbsp (45 ml) olive oil, divided

¼ tsp black pepper

6 pieces **pancetta** style bacon, cut into 24 thin strips

2 large **zucchini**

2 tsp (10 ml) apple cider vinegar

¼ tsp salt

¼ tsp black pepper

½ c (40 g) **Parmesan cheese**, shredded

1 (250 g) package Uncle Ben's *Bistro Express* **Tomato & Herb Risotto**, prepared

If you're going to use wooden skewers for the shrimp, be sure to soak them in water for at least 20 minutes prior to grilling.

Toss the shrimp in 1 tablespoon (15 ml) olive oil to coat, and then season with black pepper. Wrap each shrimp with a strip of pancetta style bacon and then thread onto the skewers. Grill the shrimp for 5 to 7 minutes, turning halfway, until it's cooked through and the pancetta has crisped slightly.

Meanwhile, make the zucchini ribbon salad. Hold the zucchini in one hand and the vegetable peeler in the other. Make long, even strokes going down the length of the zucchini to create thin and wide ribbons. Keep slicing until you reach the seeds, then rotate the zucchini and continue making more slices until you reach the seeds.

Place the zucchini strips in a bowl, and prepare the quick vinaigrette by whisking together 2 tablespoons (30 ml) olive oil, the apple cider vinegar, salt and pepper. Drizzle the dressing over the zucchini ribbons and toss to coat. Sprinkle the Parmesan cheese over top. Serve the grilled shrimp skewers with the prepared risotto and cool zucchini ribbon salad.

Shawn's Cooking Tip: Don't throw away the zucchini cores! You can dice up the zucchini cores and use them in soups, stews and even sauces. Try stirring some diced zucchini into the meat sauce in the Pasta Balls with Meat Sauce recipe (page 87).

Variation: Instead of pancetta, try wrapping the shrimp in thin-cut bacon!

SALMON CAKES WITH SAUTÉED SUGAR SNAP PEAS

I've never seen my kids clear their plates so fast as when I make these crispy salmon cakes for them. This recipe calls for panko breadcrumbs—which I believe to be a pantry staple—to give these delicate cakes an irresistible buttery and crispy coating. Serve with a quick homemade tartar sauce and sautéed sugar snap peas. The only thing that's missing is the ocean breeze.

YIELD: 4 SERVINGS

1 lb (455 g) **salmon,** cut into tiny pieces

4 white button **mushrooms**, finely diced

¼ c (25 g) finely chopped **red bell pepper**

1 tsp garlic powder

1 tsp onion powder

2 tsp parsley flakes

¼ tsp salt

1 egg, lightly beaten

2 tbsp (30 g) mayo

1 tbsp (15 ml) **teriyaki sauce**

1 tsp white wine vinegar

⅔ c (80 g) panko breadcrumbs

½ c (60 ml) + 2 tbsp (30 ml) canola or vegetable oil, divided

1 lb (455 g) **sugar snap peas,** trimmed and stringed

2 cloves garlic, minced

Combine all the ingredients up to and including the panko breadcrumbs in a large bowl. Use your hands to incorporate and form into 8 equal-size patties.

Heat about ½ cup (60 ml) of oil in a pan over medium heat. Once it's hot, carefully add the salmon patties to the pan and fry for 2 to 3 minutes per side, or until the patties are a golden brown. Drain on a paper towel–lined plate and keep warm.

Meanwhile, heat 2 tablespoons (30 ml) of oil in a wok or large skillet over medium-high heat. Toss in the sugar snap peas and cook, stirring occasionally until peas are crisp-tender, about 4 minutes. Toss in the garlic and cook for an additional 1 to 2 minutes or until the garlic becomes fragrant. Season with salt and pepper to taste and serve alongside the salmon cakes.

Shawn's Quick Tip: To save time on chopping and dicing, just place all the ingredients for the salmon cakes in a large food processor, pulse until it comes together and shape into patties.

Variation: What's a salmon cake without a tangy tarter sauce?! Whisk together 2 tablespoons (30 ml) mayo, 1 tablespoon (15 ml) sour cream, 1 tablespoon (15 g) pickle relish, ½ teaspoon horseradish, ¼ teaspoon salt and ⅛ teaspoon black pepper. Keep it chilled until ready to enjoy!

SPICY GRILLED SALMON WITH A CRISP ASIAN SALAD

Grilling salmon can be a little intimidating, but it's actually a fantastic way to cook this hearty fish. Make sure your grill rack is brushed down with olive oil, and remember that the salmon will continue to cook when it's taken off the grill. My husband's famous advice: "You can always cook it longer, but you can't cook it less." You'll know your salmon is ready when it's turned from translucent to an opaque color and flakes easily.

YIELD: 4 SERVINGS

1 c (100 g) **sugar snap peas**, sliced thinly lengthwise

8 button **mushrooms**, thinly sliced

1 **red bell pepper,** thinly sliced

2 tbsp (30 ml) **teriyaki sauce**

¼ c (60 ml) rice wine vinegar

2 tbsp (2 g) chopped cilantro, optional

Olive oil

4 (1-inch [2.5 cm] thick) **salmon** steaks

Salt and pepper

1 tsp chipotle chili powder, or regular chili powder

Prepare the crisp salad by combining the sliced sugar snap peas, sliced mushrooms and bell peppers in a bowl. In a small bowl, whisk together the teriyaki sauce and rice wine vinegar. Toss the mixture with the veggies and optional chopped cilantro. Keep chilled until ready to serve.

Heat your grill/grill pan to medium heat, then brush the rack/pan with olive oil.

Season each side of the salmon steaks with salt, pepper and chipotle chili powder, then drizzle with a little olive oil. Wait till the grill is hot in order to ensure a nice sear on the salmon. Grill for about 3 to 4 minutes on the first side, then carefully flip and grill for an additional 2 to 3 minutes.

Serve the spicy grilled salmon with a side of the cool and crisp Asian vegetable salad.

Shawn's Tip: Keep the salmon lightly covered in foil until ready to serve. The steam will help keep the salmon moist and delicious!

TERIYAKI SALMON POUCHES

Parchment pouches are a fantastic way to cook salmon, or any type of fish really, because the delicate fish won't stick to the parchment. Plus it cuts down on dishes, which is a serious bonus for me, and it also results in perfectly moist, steamed fish and veggies every time!

YIELD: 4 SERVINGS

4 **salmon** filets, skin removed

4 tsp (20 ml) olive oil

Salt and pepper

1 c (100 g) **sugar snap peas**

2 c (140 g) sliced **mushrooms**

1 **red bell pepper**, sliced

½ c (120 ml) **teriyaki sauce**

¼ c (85 g) honey

2 tbsp (30 ml) rice vinegar

1 tsp ginger powder

1 tsp sesame oil

½ tsp crushed red pepper flakes

Optional, for serving: white rice

Preheat the oven to 400°F (205°C), and place a large baking sheet on the bottom rack.

Make two small slices on the top of each salmon filet, but not deep enough to cut through. Drizzle each filet with 1 teaspoon olive oil and season with salt and pepper. Place each salmon inside a parchment cooking bag—found near the foils and plastic wraps—then top each with ¼ cup (25 g) sugar snap peas, ½ cup (35 g) sliced mushrooms and ¼ of the sliced red bell pepper strips.

Combine the remaining ingredients in a small bowl and whisk together. Drizzle over the salmon and veggies, reserving ¼ cup (60 ml) for later. Seal up the pouches by folding the opening closed several times, then carefully place on the hot baking sheet.

Bake for 20 minutes, then transfer each pouch to serving plates. Cut open the top, being careful of the escaping steam, and drizzle just a little more teriyaki sauce on top. Enjoy!

These flavors beg to be served on top of a bed of hot white rice!

Shawn's Tip: If you can't find the parchment cooking bags, you can make your own by folding a long piece of parchment paper in half. Unfold the parchment paper, and place the salmon and veggies on one side, then cover with the other half and fold up each side until the salmon is completely enclosed.

BAY SCALLOPS WITH A MEYER LEMON BASIL SAUCE

Get ready to feel like you're eating at a 5-star restaurant. I've locked in the flavor of these tender scallops by searing them in bacon grease—oh yes. Then I made a quick pan sauce with the combination of Meyer lemon juice and fresh basil for a bright pop of flavor that truly complements the scallops. The best way to serve this delicious dish is on top of a bed of angel hair pasta with a sprinkle of fresh Parmesan cheese. Get ready for the compliments to flow in your direction!

YIELD: 4 SERVINGS

1 ½ lb (230 g) larger **bay scallops**, patted dry with paper towels

¼ tsp salt

¼ tsp black pepper

4 strips **bacon**

¾ c (180 ml) chicken broth

1 large **Meyer lemon**, zest and juice

1 tbsp (15 ml) water

½ tsp cornstarch

1 tbsp (15 g) butter

2 tbsp (3 g) finely chopped **basil**

1 c (150 g) cherry or grape **tomatoes**, halved

8 oz (230 g) angel hair pasta, cooked according to package instructions, optional

2 oz (60 g) shredded Parmesan cheese, optional

Season the scallops with salt and pepper, and use a large skillet to cook the 4 strips of bacon until crisp. Remove the bacon from the pan, let drain on paper towels and then crumble into pieces. Drain all but 2 tablespoons (30 ml) of bacon grease from the pan and return the pan to medium heat. Sear the scallops in the bacon grease for 3 to 4 minutes per side until done. Remove the scallops from the pan and keep warm.

Add the chicken broth and Meyer lemon juice to the skillet, then bring it to a boil. Reduce the heat and simmer for 2 minutes, breaking up any browned bits from the bottom of the pan with a wooden spoon. In a small dish, combine the tablespoon (15 ml) of water with the cornstarch and stir it into the sauce.

Cook, stirring constantly until the sauce thickens slightly, then add the lemon zest, butter and basil. Taste and season with more salt and pepper if desired.

Toss the hot pasta, if using, with the halved tomatoes and serve with the scallops, sauce, crumbled bacon and a sprinkle of Parmesan cheese on top, if desired.

Shawn's Quick Tip: To quickly cut a bunch of cherry or grape tomatoes, place all the tomatoes on a plate, then place another plate on top of them, but leave a little space to cut the tomatoes. Gently press down on the plate with one hand and use a knife in your other hand to cut them all in half at the same time.

BAKED SCALLOP AND TOMATO GRATIN

I'm completely and utterly obsessed with these scallops. This is a dish that I could eat every day for the rest of my life and never get sick of it. The scallops and tomatoes are topped with a basil, garlic and lemony butter mixture, then baked until golden brown. The tomatoes just pop in your mouth and leave you begging for more. Serve this beauty with a side of crusty bread, and you'll have everyone begging for more.

YIELD: 4 SERVINGS

3 strips **bacon**, cut into small pieces

6 tbsp (90 g) butter, at room temperature

4 cloves garlic, minced

4 tbsp (6 g) fresh **basil**, minced

2 tbsp (30 ml) freshly squeezed **Meyer lemon** juice

1 tsp salt

½ tsp black pepper

6 tbsp (90 ml) olive oil

½ c (60 g) panko breadcrumbs

1 ½ lb (230 g) **bay scallops**, patted dry with paper towels

2 c (300 g) cherry or grape **tomatoes**

Preheat the oven to 425°F (219°C).

Heat a skillet over medium heat and cook the bacon just until it starts to render—about 3 to 4 minutes—then drain on a paper towel–lined plate. Make the butter topping by combining the soft butter, bacon, garlic, basil, Meyer lemon juice, salt and pepper in the bowl of your stand mixer fitted with the paddle attachment. Once the butter mixture is combined, turn the mixer to low and slowly stream in the olive oil. Use a spoon to fold in the breadcrumbs.

Divide the scallops and tomatoes between 4 gratin dishes—or you can place them all in one pie pan to make it more family style. Place the gratin dishes on a baking sheet to make it easier to put in and take out of the oven. Spoon the butter mixture on top of the scallops and tomatoes and bake for 10 to 12 minutes. Finish it with a quick 2-minute broil to brown the tops and serve warm with a side of crusty bread!

Shawn's Tip: If you're having a hard time finding Meyer Lemons, regular lemons will work for this recipe too.

BACON-WRAPPED BAY SCALLOPS WITH A TOMATO BASIL SALAD

When my husband and I go out on dates, we like to order two appetizers and split a dinner—*yes, we're 87 years old.* One of our favorite restaurants has these bacon-wrapped scallops that my husband always orders, so I was inspired to make my own at home. Let's just say my husband prefers eating these at home now, especially with this tomato basil salad alongside. I love throwing the tomato basil mixture on top of some leafy greens, and then popping the bacon-wrapped scallops on top to make one giant salad.

YIELD: 4 SERVINGS

1 ½ lb (230 g) **bay scallops**, patted dry with paper towels

½ tsp salt

¼ tsp black pepper

¼ tsp smoked paprika

10 strips **bacon**, cut into thirds

2 c (300 g) cherry or grape **tomatoes**, halved

2 tbsp (3 g) **basil**, cut into ribbons

2 tbsp (30 ml) **Meyer lemon** juice

4 tbsp (60 ml) olive oil

2 cloves garlic, minced

8 wooden skewers

Preheat the oven to 425°F (219°C).

Soak the wooden skewers in water for 20 minutes, then line a baking sheet with foil, and place an oven-safe rack on top of the foil.

Season both sides of the scallops with salt, pepper and smoked paprika. Wrap each scallop with a small slice of bacon, then thread the scallops onto the skewers, leaving space between each scallop to allow the bacon to crisp up. Place the skewers on the rack and bake for 20 minutes. Flip them over and bake for an additional 15 minutes, or until the bacon has fully cooked. Keep an eye on them because some bacon can cook faster than others, so make sure they don't burn.

Meanwhile, prepare the tomato basil salad by combining the tomatoes and basil in a bowl. Whisk together the Meyer lemon juice, olive oil and garlic, and season to taste with salt and pepper. Pour over the tomatoes and toss to coat. Serve the salad chilled with the bacon-wrapped scallops.

Shawn's Tip: You could also use the larger sea scallops in this recipe, just make sure to remove the membrane around the scallops and pat them dry before seasoning.

EAST MEETS WEST HALIBUT CEVICHE

Back when my husband and I were still freshly married, he convinced me that he *neeeeeded* to go on a weeklong fishing trip with his brothers to Alaska. I was hesitant at first to let him go, but when he assured me he would bring back some fresh salmon and halibut, I was more than willing to send him on his way. He brought home more than 100 pounds (45 kg) of fish. Needless to say, our freezer was stocked for a full year! I quickly became skilled in the ways of preparing halibut. Ceviche was, and still is, one of my favorite ways to use the halibut. What is so awesome about ceviche is that the halibut is actually cooked by the acidity of the lime juice, which is perfect for those hot days when you don't want to turn the stove on. Serve this light and refreshing meal with crispy corn tortilla chips, and you'll be hooked!

YIELD: 6 SERVINGS

1 lb (455 g) **halibut**, cut into small bite-size pieces

1 c (240 ml) **lime** juice

½ **red onion**, finely chopped

2 **mangos**, diced

2-3 tbsp (30-45 ml) **Thai sweet chili sauce**

½ c (8 g) chopped cilantro

Salt

Corn tortilla chips or tostada shells, optional

Place the halibut in a shallow glass dish, cover with the lime juice and let sit for 20 minutes, or until the halibut is no longer raw.

Combine the remaining ingredients in a large bowl. Drain and discard the lime juice from the halibut, add the halibut to the mango mixture and gently stir it in to combine. Serve the chilled ceviche with chips or on top of tostada shells.

Shawn's Tip: Don't skimp on the lime juice here. Be sure to squeeze fresh limes rather than using the bottled variety. The acidity in fresh limes is more potent than the bottled stuff.

GRILLED HALIBUT TACOS WITH THAI MANGO SALSA

The first time I tasted Thai sweet chili sauce, I was instantly hooked. It's been a staple in my fridge for years now, and I'm certain that once you try it, you'll keep it stocked too. Bring the taste of the tropics to the table with these mouthwatering Halibut Tacos! If you're not feeling like tacos, use the grilled halibut and Thai mango salsa on top of a bed of leafy greens for a light supper. Either way you serve it, you're really going to enjoy the combination of this flaky fish with sweet mango salsa.

YIELD: 4 SERVINGS

2 tbsp (30 ml) olive oil
5 tbsp (75 ml) **lime** juice, divided
1 tsp garlic powder
Salt and pepper
1 lb (455 g) **halibut** filets
2 **mangos**, diced
½ c (100 g) **red onion**, diced
2 tbsp (30 ml) **Thai sweet chili sauce**
2 tbsp (2 g) chopped cilantro
Tortillas, optional
Shredded purple cabbage, optional

Combine the olive oil, 4 tablespoons (60 ml) lime juice, garlic powder, salt and pepper to taste and halibut in a zip-tip bag and let marinate on the counter for 10 minutes. Heat the grill to medium and brush the grill rack with olive oil to prevent sticking. Grill the halibut filets for 3 to 4 minutes per side, or until the halibut easily flakes.

Meanwhile combine the diced mangos, red onion, 1 tablespoon (15 ml) lime juice, Thai sweet chili sauce, cilantro and salt to taste in a small bowl. Serve the warm grilled halibut on top of warm tortillas with shredded cabbage if using, some of the Thai mango salsa and a slice of lime on the side.

Variation: Give the Thai mango salsa a sweet twist by adding ½ cup (60 g) of dried cranberries that have been soaked in 2 cups (480 ml) hot water for 20 minutes.

SWEET AND SPICY HALIBUT MANGO STIR-FRY

This stir-fry is so bright and colorful, and I just love how the flavor of the mango intensifies when it's warmed up with the halibut. We serve this quick fresh dinner over a bed of white rice and garnish with some chopped green onions.

YIELD: 4 SERVINGS

2 tbsp (30 ml) olive oil, divided

1 lb (455 g) **halibut**, cut into 1-inch (2.5 cm) pieces

¼ tsp salt

⅛ tsp black pepper

½ large **red onion**, chopped

1 tsp garlic salt

2 tbsp (30 ml) **lime** juice

4 tbsp (60 ml) **Thai sweet chili sauce**

1 **mango**, diced

4 c (700 g) prepared white rice, optional

2 tbsp (10 g) diced green onions, optional

Heat 1 tablespoon (15 ml) olive oil over medium heat in a large wok or skillet. Season the halibut with salt and pepper and sear in the hot skillet on each side for 1 to 2 minutes, or until cooked through. Once cooked, move from the skillet to a plate and keep warm.

Return the skillet to the stovetop and add the remaining 1 tablespoon (15 ml) olive oil. Sauté the onion until tender, and then add the garlic salt, lime juice and sweet chili sauce to the wok, stirring to combine. Cook for 2 minutes, stirring often, then add the mango and halibut to the skillet and stir to incorporate and heat through. Season with salt and pepper to taste, then serve immediately over warm rice and garnish with green onions, if desired.

Variation: If you can't find a good deal on halibut, try substituting with 1 pound (455 g) peeled and deveined raw shrimp.

Shawn's Tip: If you want to up the spice factor, try adding a pinch of crushed red pepper flakes to the pan when you add the lime juice.

SPICY SHRIMP, CORN AND POTATO BISQUE

Whenever I hear the word "bisque," I'm immediately transported back to the short trip my family and I took one summer to Ketchikan, Alaska. We took an 8-hour ferry ride to this small port town where we played the classic tourist: browsing shops, snapping photos and of course, eating. We found an amazing restaurant inside this one hotel that is strategically placed on the mountainside. The only way up to the restaurant was by way of a sideways elevator that boasted amazing views of the bay on your way up. We ordered everything seafood, including an amazing seafood bisque. I've created a simple and quick version of my own here, with just a bit of southwestern flair to keep you going back for more.

YIELD: 6 SERVINGS

1 tbsp (15 ml) olive oil

1 medium onion, chopped

1 clove garlic, minced

4 c (950 ml) chicken broth

1 tbsp (6 g) **chipotle chiles in adobo sauce**, remove seeds to lessen the spice

1 lb (455 g) **creamer potatoes**, cut into 1-inch (2.5 cm) pieces

1 c (240 ml) **half and half**

2 c (330 g) **frozen corn**, thawed

1 lb (455 g) medium **shrimp**, peeled and deveined

½ tsp salt

¼ tsp black pepper

Heat a large Dutch oven over medium heat and add the olive oil. Sauté the onion and garlic until tender and fragrant. Add the broth, chipotle chiles and potatoes to the pot and bring to a boil. Reduce the heat to a simmer and cook for 10 to 12 minutes, until the potatoes are tender.

Carefully transfer the mixture to a blender or food processor and blend until smooth. Then return to the Dutch oven over low heat. Stir in the half and half and add the corn and shrimp to the pot. Increase the heat to medium and cook, stirring occasionally, until the shrimp are cooked through, about 5 minutes. Season with salt and pepper, taste and adjust seasonings as needed.

Shawn's Kitchen Tip: I never use a full can of chipotle chiles, so to prevent waste, I divide and freeze the chiles with a little of the sauce in an ice cube tray. Pop them out when they're frozen, store them in a zip-top bag in your freezer and defrost just one at a time when needed!

SKILLET SHRIMP, CORN AND POTATOES WITH A CREAMY CHIPOTLE SAUCE

I'm sure you've figured out by now that I have an undying love for skillet meals. I especially love skillet meals that come together quickly and effortlessly plus pack a bunch of big bold flavors. This is definitely one of those meals. By microwaving the potatoes before pan-roasting them, you save tons of time. It's one of my weeknight dinner hacks that always comes in handy. You'll especially love the creamy chipotle sauce that's drizzled on top; it adds the perfect amount of spice to this zesty dinner!

YIELD: 4 SERVINGS

½ of a **chipotle chile pepper**

½ tsp **adobo sauce**

3 tbsp (45 g) mayonnaise

1 tbsp (15 ml) **half and half**

1 lb (455 g) medium **shrimp**, peeled and deveined

2 tbsp (30 ml) olive oil, divided

1 lb (455 g) **creamer potatoes**, cut into 1-inch (2.5 cm) pieces

2 cups (330 g) **frozen corn**, thawed

½ tsp salt

⅛ tsp pepper

Place the chipotle chile pepper—remove the seeds to lessen the intensity of heat—adobo sauce, mayonnaise and half and half in a blender or food processor. Pulse a few times until well blended. Add more half and half to thin the sauce, or more mayonnaise to thicken it to your desired preference. Set aside for later use.

Season the shrimp on both sides with salt and pepper. Add 1 tablespoon (15 ml) of olive oil to a heavy bottomed skillet—I prefer to use my castiron skillet—over medium heat. Add the shrimp and sauté until they turn pink and are cooked through, approximately 3 to 4 minutes, turning once halfway. Remove the shrimp from the skillet to a warm plate and keep warm.

Meanwhile, place the potatoes in a microwave-safe bowl and cover with plastic wrap. Microwave on high power for 5 minutes to quickly soften the potatoes. Add another tablespoon (15 ml) of olive oil to the skillet and toss the warmed potatoes, thawed corn, salt and pepper into the hot skillet and sauté, stirring occasionally, until the potatoes have browned. Add the shrimp back to the pan and stir to combine. Serve with a drizzle of the creamy chipotle sauce on top.

Bulk It Up With: Try adding ½ of a diced onion and 1 small, diced zucchini. Just toss the extra veggies in the skillet along with the potatoes and corn and proceed with the recipe.

HOME-STYLE SHRIMP BOWLS

Back when my husband and I were first married and I was just learning the ins and outs of the kitchen, a friend of mine invited us over for a fancy dinner. She assigned me to make mashed potatoes, and I told her that I had the tastiest instant potatoes in my pantry. She looked at me like I had three eyeballs. I took a deep breath and attempted homemade mashed potatoes for the first time. I was thoroughly annoyed with having to peel each and every potato, but I managed. Over the years, I've discovered that certain types of potatoes have amazingly thin skins that do not require you to peel them—bonus points for extra nutrients in the peels! Creamer potatoes are one of those varieties, as well as reds. I love this Home-Style Shrimp Bowl because it feels like true comfort food to me—creamy mashed potatoes, spiced-up buttery corn and roasted shrimp on top.

YIELD: 4 SERVINGS

2 lb (910 g) **creamer potatoes**

1 c (240 ml) **half and half**

6 tbsp (90 g) butter, divided

1 ¼ tsp garlic powder, divided

½ tsp salt

¼ tsp black pepper

1 lb (455 g) medium **shrimp**, peeled and deveined

1 tbsp (15 ml) olive oil

1 tsp cumin

1 tsp **adobo sauce**

Salt and pepper

2 c (330 g) **frozen corn**, thawed

½ tbsp (3 g) **chipotle chiles in adobo sauce**, minced

Preheat the oven to 400°F (205°C).

Place the potatoes in a large pot of water and bring to a boil. Cook until the potatoes are fork-tender, about 12 minutes, then drain and return to the pot. Add the half and half, 3 tablespoons (45 g) of butter, ¼ teaspoon garlic powder, ½ teaspoon salt and ¼ teaspoon black pepper. Then use a potato masher to mash the potatoes to your desired consistency, and keep warm.

Place the shrimp in a large bowl and add the olive oil, cumin, 1 teaspoon garlic powder, adobo sauce and salt and pepper. Coat the shrimp in the mixture and then place on a parchment-lined baking sheet and bake for 6 to 8 minutes, until fully cooked.

Meanwhile, heat a large skillet over the stove and add the remaining 3 tablespoons (45 g) of butter. Toss in the corn and chipotle chiles, stirring to cook through and char slightly, seasoning with salt and pepper to taste. Divide the mashed potatoes among 4 bowls, and top with the spicy corn and roasted shrimp.

Variation: Add a little crunch to the party! Try preparing a 1 pound (455 g) package of crispy popcorn shrimp according to package instructions in place of the roasted shrimp.

CHAPTER FOUR:

LET'S VEG

12 SURPRISINGLY HEARTY MEATLESS MAIN DISHES

I've been a "meat and potatoes" type of girl for as long as I can remember. Meatless main dishes were something that I just couldn't wrap my head around. If it didn't contain some sort of meat, in my mind it was a side dish—that was, until I met my husband.

Growing up, his family was always extremely busy on Wednesday nights. Between church activities, sports, meetings and just life in general, Wednesdaynight dinners were always super simple: Fruit and Toast. His mother would put out a few bowls of fresh or canned fruit along with slices of buttered toast.

Obviously, I couldn't handle this. I needed something more substantial to my meals! While I do love the simplicity behind the idea, I needed my meatless meals to contain some sort of protein. That's why I really love these Quinoa and White Bean Stuffed Squash (page 146). They're super filling and extremely flavorful with the addition of the sun-dried tomatoes. Comfort meals such as Chili-Stuffed Spaghetti Squash (page 158) and Baked Spaghetti Casserole (page 169) are just a few of the many satisfying meatless recipes you'll find in this chapter!

Try one this week for "Meatless Monday," and see what you think!

QUINOA AND WHITE BEAN STUFFED SQUASH

Sometimes I find it difficult to convince my children that a meatless meal can be filling and satisfying. But with these Quinoa and White Bean Stuffed Squash, they are always pleasantly surprised at how filling they actually are. Maybe it's because they get their own roasted butternut squash that's overflowing with protein-rich white beans, bold sun-dried tomatoes and nutty quinoa? Or maybe it's because they finally started to listen to their mother—either way, I'll take it!

YIELD: 4 SERVINGS

4 small **butternut squash**, or two medium butternut squash

1 tbsp (15 ml) olive oil

Salt and pepper

1 c (170 g) **quinoa**, rainbow quinoa is pictured

2 handfuls **baby spinach**, chopped

1 (15 oz [425 g]) can **white beans**, rinsed and drained

½ c (55 g) **sun-dried tomatoes** in oil, drained, then coarsely chopped

1 tsp salt

½ tsp garlic powder

½ tsp dried parsley

¼ tsp black pepper

Preheat the oven to 425°F (219°C).

Cut the skinny tops off the 4 small butternut squash and use a spoon to scoop out the insides of the squash, creating a bowl—save the tops of the butternut squash for either the Butternut Squash Soup (page 150) or the White Bean and Quinoa Patties (page 149). If using 2 medium squash, cut them in half lengthwise and scoop out all the seeds. Brush the flesh sides of the butternut squash with olive oil and season with salt and pepper.

Place flesh-side down on a foil-lined baking sheet, then roast the small ones for 15 to 20 minutes, or medium ones for 20 to 25 minutes, until a fork can easily be inserted through the skin.

Meanwhile, bring 2 cups (480 ml) of water and the quinoa to a boil in a medium pot. Reduce the heat and simmer for 12 minutes, until the water the is absorbed. Add the remaining ingredients to the quinoa and stir until the spinach wilts and the mixture is heated through.

Turn the squash flesh-side up and stuff them with the quinoa mixture. Serve warm.

Variations: After stuffing the squash, top each with ¼ cup (30 g) of freshly shredded mozzarella and place under the broiler just until the cheese is melted and bubbly.

Other squash such as acorn, carnival and kabocha would be great alternatives to a butternut squash.

WHITE BEAN AND QUINOA PATTIES OVER A ROASTED BUTTERNUT SQUASH AND SPINACH SALAD

I love the bright colors of this gorgeous salad. Not only is it so pretty to look at, but it also tastes amazing! The quick sun-dried tomato vinaigrette drizzled on top of the crispy white bean and quinoa patties give it just the right amount of pop, while the roasted butternut squash brings it all back down to earth. I just know this salad is going to put a smile on your face.

YIELD: 4 SERVINGS

1 (2 lb [910 g]) **butternut squash**, halved lengthwise and seeds removed

1 tbsp (15 ml) olive oil

Salt and pepper

½ cup (85 g) **quinoa**

1 (15 oz [425 g]) can **white beans**, rinsed and drained

¼ c (25 g) **sun-dried tomatoes** in oil, drained and patted dry

½ tsp salt

¼ tsp black pepper

1 tbsp (1 g) dried parsley

1 tsp garlic powder

1 egg

3 tbsp (45 ml) olive oil

6 oz (170 g) **baby spinach**

FOR THE SUN-DRIED TOMATO VINAIGRETTE

¼ c (25 g) **sun-dried tomatoes** in oil + ¼ c (60 ml) of the oil

2 tbsp (30 ml) white wine vinegar

¼ tsp salt

⅛ tsp black pepper

Preheat the oven to 425°F (219°C). Brush the flesh sides of the butternut squash with olive oil and season with salt and pepper. Place flesh-side down on a foil-lined baking sheet, then roast for 20 to 25 minutes, until a fork can easily be inserted through the skin.

Meanwhile, bring 1 cup (240 ml) of water and the quinoa to a boil in a small pot. Reduce the heat and simmer for 12 minutes, until the water is absorbed. Let cool for 10 minutes.

Add the white beans, sun-dried tomatoes, salt, pepper, dried parsley and garlic powder to a food processor. Pulse several times until the mixture is combined. Add the quinoa and egg and pulse a few more times until completely mixed. Shape the white bean mixture into 8 equal-size patties (about ½ inch [1.3 cm] thick and 2 inches [5 cm] in diameter). Heat the oil in a heavy skillet over medium-high heat. Add the patties to the skillet and cook for 2 to 3 minutes per side, until golden brown.

To make the sun-dried tomato vinaigrette, combine the ingredients in a blender and puree until fully blended.

Cube the roasted butternut squash and serve over a bed of spinach with the warm white bean and quinoa patties. Drizzle the sun-dried tomato vinaigrette over top.

Shawn's Cooking Tip: The patties can be prepared up to a day in advance, by storing the uncooked patties in the fridge. Just heat the oil in the skillet and finish cooking them right before serving.

ROASTED BUTTERNUT SQUASH AND SUN-DRIED TOMATO SOUP WITH TOASTED QUINOA

This hearty soup is warm and inviting with its creamy and smooth butternut squash base and wilted baby spinach swirled throughout. But what really gets me are the fun and crunchy toasted quinoa sprinkled on top. The quinoa gives off a delightful nutty aroma when lightly toasted in a skillet. It's extremely difficult to keep your hands out of it! Just make sure you save some for the soup!

YIELD: 6 SERVINGS

4 tbsp (60 g) butter

1 c (260 g) canned **white beans**, drained and rinsed

½ tsp garlic powder

⅔ c (75 g) **sun-dried tomatoes** in oil, drained

6 c (840 g) peeled and cubed **butternut squash**

7 c (1 ¾ L) vegetable broth

½ c (85 g) uncooked **quinoa**

1 tsp Italian Seasoning

3 c (90 g) **baby spinach**, coarsely chopped

Salt and pepper

Melt the butter in a large Dutch oven over medium heat. Add the white beans and garlic powder to the Dutch oven and sauté for 2 minutes. Add the sun-dried tomatoes, butternut squash and vegetable broth. Bring the mixture to a boil, then reduce the heat to small boil and cook, stirring occasionally for 20 to 25 minutes, or until the squash is very tender.

Meanwhile, soak the quinoa in 2 cups (480 ml) of warm water for 5 minutes, before draining and shaking off as much excess water as possible. Heat a medium skillet over medium-high heat and add the quinoa to the dry pan. Keep stirring the quinoa until all the moisture has cooked out and the quinoa starts to toast and turn a light golden brown. The quinoa will pop a little, almost like popcorn, while it's toasting. Remove the toasted quinoa from the skillet to a paper towel–lined plate to cool. Set aside.

Use an immersion blender—or blend the soup in batches in a standing blender—to puree the soup until smooth and creamy. Stir in the Italian seasoning and baby spinach until it wilts and then season with salt and pepper to taste. Serve with a sprinkle or two of the toasted quinoa on top.

Shawn's Quick Tip: Use a vegetable peeler to quickly and efficiently peel the skin off the butternut squash before halving the squash to remove its seeds.

CREAMY MUSHROOM STROGANOFF

You'll never miss the beef with this creamy and delicious meatless dinner. Egg noodles are tossed in a cheesy and creamy sauce then topped with sautéed mini portobello mushrooms, onions and poblano peppers for the ultimate comfort meal. My kids are obsessed with mushrooms, so whenever I make this dish for them, they can't get enough of it!

YIELD: 4 SERVINGS

4 c (480 g) medium egg noodles

1 tsp olive oil

1 medium **onion**, diced

1 **poblano pepper**, seeded and diced

4 c (300 g) **portobello mushrooms**, sliced

2 tbsp (30 g) butter

2 tbsp (15 g) flour

2 tbsp (30 ml) dry sherry cooking wine, optional

1 ½ c (355 ml) milk

½ tsp salt

¼ tsp pepper

1 c (115 g) **Monterey Jack cheese**

½ c (115 g) **sour cream**

2 tbsp (2 g) chopped parsley, optional

Cook the noodles according to the package instructions.

Meanwhile, heat the olive oil in a large skillet or Dutch oven, over medium-high heat. Toss in the onion and pepper and sauté for 1 minute, then add the mushrooms and cook until they soften, about 3 minutes, stirring frequently. Move the mushroom mixture from the pan to a plate or bowl and keep warm.

Use a paper towel to quickly wipe out the pan and return the pan to the stove over medium heat. Add the butter and let it melt, then whisk in the flour so there are no clumps. Add the dry sherry, if using, and gradually add the milk, still whisking to prevent clumps. Once all the milk has been added, stir in the salt, pepper and Monterey Jack cheese until the cheese melts. Remove the pan from the heat and stir in the sour cream and cooked egg noodles.

Serve the noodles with the mushroom mixture on top and garnish with chopped parsley if desired.

Shawn's Quick Tip: Look for a pre-sliced mushroom blend if you can't find mini portobello mushrooms to save time on chopping and slicing.

CHEESY PORTOBELLO STUFFED POBLANOS

This is basically a quick version of one of my Mexican favorites—Chile Relleno. We're taking the time to roast, sweat, peel and stuff some poblano peppers, but trust me, it's really not that difficult. By roasting them all under the broiler of your oven, you're going to save loads of time. Rather than dipping these stuffed peppers in an egg batter and frying them, we're baking them casserole-style for an easy weeknight dinner your whole family will love! Try serving these with a side of Spanish Rice (page 33) for a complete meal.

YIELD: 6 SERVINGS

6 **poblano peppers**

1 tsp olive oil

1 **onion**, diced

2 **portobello mushrooms**, stems removed and diced

2 ½ c (285 g) shredded **Monterey Jack cheese**

1 tsp garlic powder

½ tsp cumin

½ tsp chili powder

½ tsp salt

Pepper

½ cup (115 g) **sour cream**

Optional toppings: diced tomatoes, freshly chopped cilantro, hot sauce

Place the peppers under your oven's broiler for 2 minutes per side, until the peppers have blackened and charred. Remove the peppers from the oven and place in a bowl covered with plastic wrap. Let the peppers steam in the bowl for at least 5 minutes, then peel all the plastic-like skin from the peppers and discard.

Carefully make a 2-inch (5 cm) slit in one side of the peppers and remove the seeds, leaving an open cavity in the peppers. Place the peppers, cut-side up, in a casserole dish and set aside.

Heat the oven to 375°F (191°C).

Heat the olive oil in a skillet and sauté the onion for 2 minutes, then add the diced mushrooms and sauté for 2 extra minutes. Pour the mushroom mixture into a bowl with the cheese, garlic powder, cumin, chili powder, salt, pepper and sour cream. Stir to combine.

Stuff this mixture into each pepper and bake for 15 minutes or until the cheese is melted and bubbly. Serve with extra sour cream, diced tomatoes and fresh cilantro if desired.

Shawn's Cooking Tip: Make sure you properly clean the portobello mushrooms before slicing. To do this, you'll want to remove the stem and discard it. Use a spoon to scrape out the dark gills underneath the cap of the mushroom and discard those as well. Use a damp paper towel to wipe the caps to remove any dirt or debris. Now you're all set to get dicing!

Variation: Try spicing up the peppers even more by using a Pepper Jack cheese instead of the Monterey Jack cheese.

PORTOBELLO AND POBLANO FAJITAS

Several years ago, I worked at a popular restaurant chain as a server. One of my favorite things on the menu was their steak and poblano fajitas. I've gone ahead and made a meatless variation of it, and trust me, you'll never miss the steak! One major bonus is that these fajitas are prepared in one pan, which means fewer dishes to clean, and that's always a win in my book! For tips on how to properly clean the portobello mushrooms, be sure to check out the notes on page 154.

YIELD: 4 SERVINGS

1 tbsp (15 ml) olive oil

½ tsp chili powder

½ tsp cumin

½ tsp garlic powder

¼ tsp salt

2 **portobello mushrooms**, sliced into strips

1 **poblano pepper**, sliced into strips

1 **medium onion**, sliced into strips

8 small tortillas

1 c (115 g) shredded **Monterey Jack cheese**

½ c (115 g) **sour cream**

Optional toppings: lime wedges, cilantro, diced tomatoes, guacamole

Combine the first 5 ingredients in a large zip-top bag and shake. Add the mushrooms, pepper and onion to the bag and gently shake to coat.

Heat a large cast iron or heavy-bottomed skillet over medium-high heat. Once the skillet is nice and hot, pour the mushroom and pepper mixture into the skillet and sauté, stirring occasionally, until the peppers and onions have charred slightly and the mushrooms are tender.

Serve the fajita mixture immediately on the tortillas topped with cheese and sour cream, along with any optional toppings you desire.

Variation: Give these fajitas a little extra zip when you drizzle them with a cilantro-based Chimichurri sauce (page 91).

CHILI-STUFFED SPAGHETTI SQUASH

Is there anything more comforting than a big bowl of noodles and chili covered in cheese and baked to bubbly melted perfection? I've "healthified" my favorite comfort food by roasting some spaghetti squash in the oven until it's so tender that it's practically falling out of its shell. Then I stuffed it full of sautéed veggies and warm vegetarian chili and placed a generous helping of shredded marbled cheddar on top—okay, so maybe that's not the healthiest, but c'mon, just look at how delicious this looks! Depending on the size of the spaghetti squash you choose, these can be very generous portions. I usually split one halved squash between two of my kids.

YIELD: 4 SERVINGS

2 tbsp (30 ml) olive oil, divided

2 small to medium size **spaghetti squash**, halved lengthwise and seeds removed

Salt and pepper

1 **onion**, diced

1 **green bell pepper**, diced

2 (15 oz [425 g] each) cans **vegetarian style chili**

2 c (230 g) shredded **marbled cheddar cheese**

2 tbsp (2 g) chopped cilantro, optional

Preheat the oven to 425°F (219°C). Use 1 tablespoon (15 ml) of olive oil to brush the fleshy insides of the spaghetti squash, and season with salt and pepper. Place the squash flesh-side down on a foil-lined baking sheet and roast in the oven for 40 to 45 minutes, until the squash is super tender.

Meanwhile, add the remaining tablespoon (15 ml) of olive oil to a large skillet and sauté the diced onion and bell pepper over medium heat until tender, about 4 minutes. Pour the chili into the pan and heat through.

When the squash is cooked, carefully turn them flesh-side up so they look like long bowls, and use a fork to gently shred the insides of the squash, leaving about ¼ inch (6 mm) of squash intact. Stuff the squash with the chili mixture and then top with the shredded cheese. Return the squash to the oven and bake for 5 minutes, until the cheese is fully melted and slightly bubbles around the edges.

Serve inside the squash, garnished with the chopped cilantro if desired.

Variation: Make it an Italian favorite by switching out the chili for 3 cups (710 ml) of marinara sauce, and using 2 cups (230 g) of mozzarella cheese instead of marbled cheddar.

SAVORY SPAGHETTI SQUASH WAFFLES TOPPED WITH CHILI

I think it should be on everyone's bucket list to try a savory waffle. Don't get confused by the shape; these waffles are not sweet, but rather stuffed with peppers, onions, cheese and oh yes—spaghetti squash! I quickly steamed this squash in the microwave, but you could definitely use the roasting method from the Chili-Stuffed Spaghetti Squash (page 158) to give it more of that roasted flavor. Whatever you do, be sure to pile these waffles with chili and extra cheese!

YIELD: 4 SERVINGS

1 medium **spaghetti squash**

1 tsp olive oil

½ **onion**, diced

½ **green bell pepper**, diced

2 eggs

⅓ c (65 g) flour

½ tsp salt

⅛ tsp pepper

1 tsp chili powder

1 c (115 g) shredded **marbled cheddar cheese** + extra for serving if desired

1 (15 oz [425 g]) can **vegetarian style chili**

Optional toppings: sour cream, diced green onions, hot sauce

Quickly steam the spaghetti squash in your microwave by slicing the squash in half, lengthwise, and cleaning out the seeds. Place half of the squash, flesh-side up, in a microwave-safe dish, then fill the squash with water. Place the other half of the squash, flesh-side down, on top of the water-filled squash. Carefully put it in the microwave and cook on high power for 10 minutes. Drain any excess water and use a fork to shred the squash. Measure out 3 ½ cups (525 g) of squash and reserve the rest for a later use.

Add the olive oil to a skillet, and sauté the onion and bell pepper until soft and tender, about 3 minutes. Remove from the heat.

In a large bowl, whisk the eggs for 1 minute, until they become pale yellow and a little frothy. Whisk in the flour, salt, pepper and chili powder and then stir for 30 more seconds. Add the squash, peppers and onions to the mixture and stir to combine. Finally add the shredded cheese and stir to combine.

Pour ½ cup (120 ml) of the mixture onto a lightly-greased, hot waffle iron and close. Let the waffles cook for 3 to 4 minutes before carefully removing from the waffle iron. Keep them warm until ready to serve.

Prepare the chili according to can's instructions, and top the waffles with hot chili and extra cheese if desired. Top with any optional toppings you like.

Variation: Turn your spaghetti squash waffle into a spaghetti squash cornbread by adding ⅓ cup (50 g) of yellow cornmeal to the batter in addition to the ⅓ cup (65 g) flour.

SLOW COOKER SPAGHETTI SQUASH CHILI

One of the most popular recipes on my blog is my Slow Cooker Spaghetti Squash with Meatballs.
I've taken that simple and delicious recipe and given it a meatless touch, as well as a fun Southwestern twist
that will leave you coming back for more. This is basically a "dump everything into the slow cooker
and enjoy" type of recipe that even the kids can make.

YIELD: 4 SERVINGS

1 medium **spaghetti squash**

1 **green bell pepper**, diced

1 **onion**, diced

2 (15 oz [425 g] each) cans **vegetarian style chili**

2 c (230 g) shredded **marbled cheddar cheese**

Thoroughly wash the outside of the squash and pat dry. Use a sharp knife to cut the squash in half, width-wise, and use a spoon to scoop out the seeds. Place the two halves of the squash, flesh-side down, in your slow cooker—they don't need to both touch the bottom, just shimmy them in there. Toss in the diced green bell pepper and diced onion, and then top with the two cans of chili. Cover and cook on high for 3 to 4 hours.

Carefully remove the squash from the slow cooker and place on a cutting board. Use a fork to pull the squash out of the shells. Discard the shells and return the squash to the slow cooker and stir to combine.* Serve the chili in bowls topped with shredded cheese and any other toppings you desire.

Shawn's Cooking Tip: If you find that the chili is lacking in spice after the squash is added, try adding in ½ teaspoon of chili powder to the slow cooker and stirring to combine. I'm a spice junkie, so I always enjoy mine with several dashes of hot sauce on top.

*Variation:** Instead of stirring the squash into the chili, you can optionally serve the shredded spaghetti squash on a plate topped with the chili mixture and cheese.

MEDITERRANEAN PASTA PUTTANESCA

I've always been an adventurous eater, but if there is one thing that I just cannot stand, it's capers.
I know that a classic puttanesca is brimming with pungent capers, but I took those salty beasts out and replaced
them with feta cheese. So not only do you still get that salty flavor, but it's cheeeeeesy! This hearty skillet
pasta dish will quickly become one of your family's favorite go-to meals!

YIELD: 6 SERVINGS

12 oz (340 g) uncooked whole-wheat **linguine**

¼ c (60 ml) olive oil

3 c (490 g) diced **tomatoes**

1 tsp garlic powder, or 3 cloves garlic thinly sliced

½ tsp salt

¼ tsp black pepper

1 tsp dried oregano

1 c (135 g) pitted **black olives**

1 c (230 g) marinated quartered **artichoke hearts**, drained

½ c (75 g) chopped **feta cheese**

Bring a large pot of salted water to a boil and add the linguine. While the pasta is cooking, prepare your sauce.

Heat the olive oil in a large skillet over medium heat. Add the diced tomatoes and let simmer for 30 seconds. Stir and add the garlic powder or sliced garlic, salt, pepper and oregano. Use the back of a spoon to lightly mash the tomatoes until their juices release and a sauce begins to form. Add the olives and artichokes and heat through.

Drain the pasta and add directly to the skillet, using tongs to toss the pasta in the sauce. Add the chopped feta and serve warm.

Quick Tip: Instead of chopping all the tomatoes, try using 3 cups (490 g) of canned, drained diced tomatoes plus ½ cup (120 ml) of the juice from the can.

Variation: For an even more flavorful punch, try using pitted Kalmata olives in place of the black olives.

GREEK PASTA SALAD

I'm a huge pasta salad fan. Typically I'd serve this salad as a side, but when "Meatless Monday" rolls around, I've been known to serve up extra-large portions of this yummy salad as a main dish. It's a super-quick fix that everyone is sure to love!

YIELD: 4 SERVINGS

3 c (315 g) uncooked **rotini pasta**

2 large **tomatoes,** roughly chopped

1 c (135 g) **black olives**

1 c (230 g) quartered **artichoke hearts** in oil, drained

1 c (150 g) **feta cheese,** crumbled

FOR THE DRESSING

3 tbsp (45 ml) red wine vinegar

½ tsp garlic powder

1 tsp sugar

1 tsp dried oregano

3 tbsp (45 ml) olive oil

2 tbsp (30 g) mayo

Prepare the pasta according to package instructions. Once the noodles are tender, drain them, run cold water through them until they are cooled and drain again.

Place the pasta, tomatoes, black olives, artichokes and feta in a large bowl and set aside.

In a small bowl, whisk together the ingredients for the dressing. Pour over the pasta and toss to coat. Cover and refrigerate until ready to serve, tossing again before serving.

Variation: Add a little more color to the pasta by tossing in 1 cup (90 g) of chopped green bell pepper.

BAKED SPAGHETTI CASSEROLE

One of my favorite ways to use tomatoes is to make a hearty tomato sauce. I've combined some artichoke hearts into this delicious sauce, then cooked the noodles directly in the sauce so they absorb so much of that delicious flavor. If you're using an oven-safe skillet, you can top the pasta with some crumbled feta and sliced olives and then just toss it directly into the oven to get nice and bubbly. This comforting casserole begs to be served with a side of crusty garlic bread!

YIELD: 6 SERVINGS

7 whole **tomatoes**

2 cloves garlic

1 tsp onion powder

1 tbsp (15 ml) olive oil

10 oz (285 g) uncooked whole-wheat **spaghetti noodles**

1 c (230 g) **artichoke hearts** in oil, drained and coarsely chopped

½ c (75 g) crumbled **feta cheese**

¼ c (35 g) sliced **black olives**

Optional garnish: fresh basil

Preheat the oven to 350°F (177°C).

Place the tomatoes and garlic in a large pot filled with water and bring to a boil. Cook until the tomato skins have cracked and the tomatoes are super tender. Use a slotted spoon to carefully transfer the tomatoes, garlic and ¾ cup (180 ml) of the liquid from the pot into a blender. Add the onion powder and blend until the tomato mixture is smooth.

Add the olive oil to a large skillet over medium heat. Break the spaghetti noodles into thirds and place in the hot oil, stirring to lightly toast the noodles. Pour the tomato mixture and chopped artichoke hearts into the skillet with the noodles. Bring to a small boil, and then reduce the heat to a simmer, stirring occasionally, until the pasta has absorbed most of the liquid and is tender, about 10 to 12 minutes.

Transfer the spaghetti mixture to a 3-quart (3 L) oven-safe dish. Top with the crumbled feta and sliced black olives. Bake for 10 minutes, uncovered. Let the casserole sit for 5 minutes before serving.

Variation: For a more traditional baked spaghetti, try using 1 cup (115 g) of shredded mozzarella to top the pasta before baking.

CHAPTER FIVE

A SWEET ENDING

5 INGREDIENT DESSERT RECIPES

I could probably write a whole other cookbook about 5 ingredient dessert recipes. I mean, who couldn't use that?!

I tried to hit all the dessert bases with this short chapter. There are Raspberry Cheesecake Tartlets (page 179) to quench that cheesecake craving in a matter of minutes. If you're in the mood for something soft and fluffy, give the Apple Spice Cake with Maple Cream Cheese Frosting (page 172) a try!

From cookies, to brownies and even an ice cream pie stuffed with hot fudge (page 175), you're sure to find something to satisfy your sweet tooth!

APPLE SPICE CAKE WITH MAPLE CREAM CHEESE FROSTING

You're going to fall in love with this moist and delicious Apple Spice Cake. It's filled with shredded apples and spices, then topped with a cinnamon-and-maple-infused cream cheese frosting.

YIELD: 8 TO 10 SERVINGS

1 (18 ¼ oz [520 g]) **spice cake mix**

1 (3 ½ oz [100 g]) instant vanilla **pudding** mix

4 eggs

⅓ c (80 ml) oil

1 c (240 ml) water

2 **granny smith apples**, peeled and shredded

FOR THE FROSTING

1 (16 oz [455 g]) container **cream cheese frosting**, such as Betty Crocker

½ tsp **maple extract**

¼ tsp ground cinnamon

Preheat the oven to 350°F (177°C). Lightly spray a 10" (25.5 cm) bundt pan with nonstick cooking spray and set aside.

Combine the cake mix, pudding mix, eggs, oil and water in the bowl of your stand mixer. Whisk for 30 seconds on low, then increase the speed to medium and whisk for 2 more minutes. Add the shredded apples and stir to combine. Pour the cake batter into the pan and bake for 60 to 65 minutes, or until a long wooden skewer comes out clean. Let cool for 10 minutes before removing from the pan to cool completely.

Remove the foil from the cream cheese frosting container and stir. Microwave the frosting for 10 seconds to soften. Add the maple extract and cinnamon, and then stir until completely incorporated. Frost the top of the bundt cake, letting the frosting work its way down the sides of the cake for a pretty presentation.

Shawn's Cooking Tip: To give this spice cake even more apple flavor, try substituting the water for equal amounts apple cider or apple juice!

Variation: This cake can also be prepared in a 9"x 13" (23 x 33 cm) cake pan. Bake for just 30 to 35 minutes or until toothpick inserted in the center comes out clean.

COCONUT, CASHEW AND HOT FUDGE ICE CREAM PIE

Believe it or not, one of my favorite candy bars was the inspiration for this mouthwatering ice cream pie; a chocolate bar that's infused with shredded coconut and chopped cashews. I took all those flavors and sandwiched them between two layers of vanilla ice cream and served it in a crisp chocolate graham cracker crust. Just one bite of this pie, and you'll be absolutely hooked.

YIELD: 8 SERVINGS

1 (6 oz [170 g]) premade chocolate **graham cracker pie shell**

1 ½ qt (1 ½ L) container **vanilla ice cream**, slightly softened

⅓ c (80 ml) **hot fudge** ice cream topping, plus more for drizzling

⅓ c (30 g) shredded, sweetened **coconut flakes**

½ c (70 g) **cashews**, roughly chopped

Preheat the oven to 375°F (191°C). Bake the chocolate pie shell for 6 minutes; remove from the oven and let cool completely.

Carefully spread three scoops of the softened ice cream in the base of the chocolate pie shell until it's an even layer. Pour room-temperature fudge sauce over the ice cream, and use a knife to spread into an even layer. Sprinkle the shredded coconut and cashews evenly over the top.

Use the remaining ice cream to make large scoops on top of the pie, until the whole pie is covered in scoops of ice cream. Place the pie into the freezer for at least 2 hours before slicing and serving with warm fudge sauce drizzled on top.

Variations: Try toasting the coconut before adding it to the ice cream pie for an extra nuttier flavor! Simply heat a large, dry skillet over medium heat, toss in the coconut and stir constantly until the coconut turns golden brown in color. Remove the coconut from the pan and let cool on a paper towel–lined plate before adding to the ice cream pie.

PEANUT BUTTER FUDGE BROWNIES

Get ready to take your brownies to the next level with a thick layer of peanut butter fudge and a bunch of chocolate peanut butter cups sandwiched in between! These brownies are ultra rich and chewy, and will seriously curb that chocolate and peanut butter craving.

YIELD: 16 SMALL BROWNIES

1 (18 ½ oz [525 g]) box **brownie mix—** and ingredients needed to prepare

2 c (375 g) **chocolate peanut butter cups**, such as Reese's, halved

2 c (480 g) **peanut butter morsels**, found near the chocolate chips

1 (14 oz [415 ml]) can **sweetened condensed milk**

1 tsp **vanilla extract**

Prepare your brownies according to package instructions in an 8" x 8" (20 x 20 cm) pan that has been lined with parchment paper. Leave them in the pan and let them cool completely.

Top the brownies with the halved chocolate peanut butter cups, and then prepare the simple peanut butter fudge.

Bring a small pot filled with 2 inches (5 cm) of water to a boil on the stovetop. Find a metal or glass bowl that can easily rest on top of the pot without the bottom touching the water. Add the peanut butter morsels, sweetened condensed milk and vanilla to the bowl. Stir the mixture over the boiling water until it becomes smooth. Pour the peanut butter fudge over the top of the brownies in an even layer. Let the fudge cool for at least 2 to 3 hours before slicing.

Shawn's Cooking Tip: Lining a baking pan with parchment paper makes it extremely easy to remove the baked goods from the pan once they are cool, so slicing them into the perfect size bar is a breeze!

NO BAKE RASPBERRY CHEESECAKE TARTLETS

I love the simplicity of this quick, easy and sophisticated dessert. It's the pre-made mini phyllo cups that make this recipe such a breeze. Just quickly mix up the lemon-infused cheesecake mixture, pipe it into the cups and top with a fresh raspberry! You'll be surprised at how fast these little tartlets disappear!

YIELD: 15 TARTLETS

4 oz (115 g) **cream cheese**, softened

¼ c (50 g) **sugar**

1 tsp **lemon** juice, plus 1 tsp lemon zest

15 **mini phyllo cups**, thawed, look for these in the freezer section near the desserts and pie crusts

15 fresh **raspberries**

Place the cream cheese, sugar, lemon juice and zest into a medium bowl and beat with a hand mixer until smooth and creamy. Scoop the mixture into a zip-top bag, then snip off the corner of the bag. Squeeze the cheesecake mixture into each mini phyllo cup and then top with a fresh raspberry.

Keep these stored in the fridge until ready to serve.

Variation: Use any sort of fresh berry or fruit in place of the raspberries to top these. Make them extra pretty by garnishing with small mint leaves!

CARMELITA COOKIE BARS

Delicious? Forget about it! These cookie bars are off the chain ridiculous! They're so great that even my non-sweets-eating husband frequently requests them. I started with a basic cake mix cookie, bulked it up with loads of oats and mini chocolate chips, and then I poured a silky layer of caramel right in the middle. These bars are finger licking good!

YIELD: 16 BARS

½ c (120 ml) melted butter
1 (16 ½ oz [470 g]) box yellow or white **cake mix**
2 ½ c (200 g) **quick oats**
½ c (100 g) **brown sugar**
2 eggs
1 c (170 g) mini **chocolate chips**
30 **caramel squares**, unwrapped
2 tbsp (30 ml) milk

Preheat the oven to 350°F (177°C). Line an 8" x 8" (20 x 20 cm) baking pan with parchment paper and spray with non-stick spray, then set aside.

In a large bowl, combine the melted butter, cake mix, quick oats, brown sugar and eggs. Use a sturdy wooden spoon to stir until a thick dough forms. Add the chocolate chips and stir until evenly incorporated. Press half of the dough into the prepared pan in an even layer. Bake for 10 minutes.

Meanwhile, place the unwrapped caramels in a microwave-safe bowl along with the milk and heat in the microwave on high for 30 seconds. Stir the caramels and heat for another 30 seconds. Stir and repeat until the caramels are smooth. Pour the caramel sauce on top of the base of the cookie bars. Then carefully place bits of the remaining dough on top of the caramel, covering it completely.

Bake for another 15 minutes, remove from the oven and let cool completely. Once it's come to room temperature, you can refrigerate the cookie bars to firm up the caramel even more, or keep at room temperature to enjoy a softer caramel center.

Shawn's Cooking Tip: The cookie dough can be super sticky to work with, so I recommend spraying your fingers with a nonstick spray when handling the cookie dough.

ACKNOWLEDGMENTS

I can still remember the day that I decided to create my blog, *I Wash...You Dry*. I had been pushing around the idea for a few weeks, but hadn't gotten up the courage to start it yet. I went out to lunch with two of my closest girl friends and I just blurted out, "If I write a blog about food, would you read it?" To which they both enthusiastically replied, "YES!"

My blog started out as a hobby, for friends and family to read, comment and enjoy. That hobby soon turned into a passion, and then blossomed into so much more. I had always dreamed of writing a cookbook so I could continue to share my passion for quick and easy food. The day before my 30th birthday, I received an email that would turn my dream into reality. I want to send a huge thank you to Page Street Publishing and everyone on their team for reaching out to me on that special day, listening to my crazy idea for an innovative cookbook and going for it.

Thank you to all the readers of *I Wash...You Dry* who have stuck with me over the years. Thank you for coming back again and again, making my recipes, commenting, sharing and really brightening my day with your words of encouragement.

I would like to give thanks to all my friends and family for all their love and support. Thank you for your willingness to taste test, recipe test and keep me emotionally in check during this long—*but enjoyable*—process of writing my first cookbook.

A special thank you goes out to my husband, Chris, for your amazing support, encouragement and love. Thank you for that gentle nudge to get in the kitchen and create, so many years ago. Thank you to my mother-in-law for the recipes to start me on my culinary journey. Thank you to my own mother for all your support and love and constant encouragement. You're my #1 fan, and I truly appreciate it.

Thank you to my daughter, Kaylee, and my son, Crew, for being the best dishwashers and taste testers this mom could ask for! And lastly, thank you to my younger two daughters Emma and Twila for inspiring this cookbook and for all your sweet words, praise and all the snuggles I could ever dream of. I love you all!

ABOUT THE AUTHOR

SHAWN SYPHUS launched the popular food blog, *I Wash...You Dry*, in 2010 with the goal of sharing her simple and easy recipes with family and friends. It has since attracted a large and loyal following, with her work being featured in print and on many online publications. Her work has been seen on sites such as *Better Homes and Gardens*, *Country Living*, *Women's Day*, Delish, *RedBook Magazine*, NPR, BuzzFeed, *Bon Appetit*, Pillsbury, and many more.

Once a collegiate swimmer, Shawn is now a recipe developer, writer and photographer who still enjoys keeping active by competing in triathlons and chasing after her 4 children with her husband in Southern Utah.

INDEX